Heaven Must Be Missing an Angel

 I Saw Her at the Bus Stop

Brenda Pickett Watson

ISBN 978-1-64299-363-9 (paperback)
ISBN 978-1-64299-364-6 (digital)

Christian Faith Publishing, Inc.
832 Park Avenue
Meadville, PA 16335
www.christianfaithpublishing.com

Printed in the United States of America

DEDICATIONS

To my heavenly father who I give glory and honor.

To Bobbie Frankel who said someone should
write a book about you someday.

To my husband, Charles, and family for your support

To my True Vine Baptist Church, Cleveland Institute
of Music and Shaker City Hall friends

To Lula Woodruff who inspired me to live my purpose and
her grandson Reginald Evans Jr. who designed the cover.

CONTENTS

PART 4: THE LETTERS

FOREWORD

Looking ahead, generosity is a gift among selfless people who put others before themselves. This esoteric group is generous to a fault and gives until it hurts, in which the recipient often takes it for weakness.

Brenda Pickett Watson is a member of that elite group; she has the love of God in her, which enables her to love people unconditionally.

I met her while I was working as security for the Cleveland Institute of Music years ago and she was their receptionist. She is the same Brenda Pickett Watson today as she was then.

A talented singer, Brenda was provided several opportunities to sing at Severance Hall, one of the most respected orchestras in the world, along with Central State and Cleveland's community choir for the Martin Luther King Jr. Holiday concerts several times.

Brenda Watson is a people person, her commitment and dedication to her job made her a unique asset to each and every job that she had.

Many of my acquaintances also know Brenda and they think the world of her. We all anticipate the reading of her story only as she can tell it. Will it be colorful, painful, boring, brilliant or unique? Who knows? Everybody has a story to tell.

Calvin Marshall
January 23, 2017

Part 1

JEROME SPENCER'S SCHOOL EXPERIENCE

1

ONE HOT SUMMER

It was one of the hottest summers that I could remember in Cleveland, Ohio and one of the most boring summers also. Some of the young people in the neighborhood back in the day could cut a little grass or go to the store for the widowers or older men who had some type of disability. Sometimes we made more than enough hanging out money. It was different the year of 2010. It seemed like the entire neighborhood was having financial problems. It was unreal how many people was having it so rough. Everybody was busted and disgusted.

Being a teenager was no fun. Most of the kids in my neighborhood weren't old enough to register for a work permit to work as a bagger in the grocery store. The unemployment rate was high and jobs were scarce. It seemed as though the city was on lock down. All of our regulars was either dead or just could not afford to pay us anything, so they would say, "No I don't need any help."

Crime was just beginning to get out of control. You would hear of twelve and thirteen-year-old boys and some girls stealing cars and going on joyrides. If I even thought of anything like that my mom would probably snatch the thought right out of my head. Just one look at her and you knew she didn't play; she would help them lock your butt up, and wouldn't come to see you or waste her hard-earned money on a loser.

She said it all the time whenever she heard that somebody had done such a stupid thing, especially a kid. I also couldn't hang out with anyone with that type of mindset. Mom checked out everyone that I hung out with. She had to know where they lived and who were their parents, and, the most important thing, where are they employed, if they were employed. "Dang, Mom," Rome said to his mother. "Why do you have to know all of that?"

Her reasoning was that if a person can't afford some of the things that we had, they might get tempted and take something from the house and I would be so upset. We did not have much, but it was ours.

We were doing okay. My mother made certain that the family's basic human necessities, such as food, clothing, utilities, and a mortgage were met. Never the less, we were not able to afford much extra and we definitely couldn't afford to lose anything. She was a good mother and didn't mind at all if our friends hung out around our house. She had two jobs, one in house cleaning and one as an assistant cook in a hospital. The girl could throw down. She was a good cook but the hospital didn't pay that much for assistant cooks.

If she had a chance to take some classes and get her license, she could have been head cook. She just couldn't afford it and she didn't want to leave us at home alone all the time. She felt guilty with the two jobs even though we understood the situation.

My dad was already in the DDC, as me and my boys called it: The Divorce Dad Club. Most of the kids in the neighborhood had parents who were divorced. All except Leroy Jackson. His parents were still together. From how he would brag, his father would not be joining the club anytime soon. He was good to his mom and they spent a lot of time together.

This one hot Friday, around twelve, Tyrone, Leroy, and I met up as usual just to hang out. Leroy was the only one who had a bike. Leroy was the only one who had anything even though he was a little selfish most of the time. When we all would put up for a pizza to split he would always cry broke. Then we would see him later that day with a bag of stuff from the corner store. There he was, riding on that big, shiny, apple-red bike knowing that we—especially me—wanted to ride it. He was across the street while we were trying to figure out where we would get at least five dollars. Five would get us a bag of stuff at this store that had penny candy still and a bag of chips for twenty-five cents. Leroy asked, "What yawl up to?" like he didn't know.

Tyrone had to be desperate in order for him to ask Leroy for a loan. That was something he did not like to do. It felt more like begging. Now, Tyrone is not a beggar. He had a lot of pride, so, I knew he really wanted something.

"How you going to pay me back next week you don't have a job?" Leroy asked. We knew what that meant: He was not going to help us out.

"OK, be that way," I said to Leroy then turned to Tyrone. "Let's go in the store. Maybe Mr. Knuckles is in a good mood and just might be nice enough to give us some credit today."

Mr. Knuckles would always say the same thing Leroy said, "How you going to pay me back? You don't have jobs. You don't even get an allowance. Get out of here."

We heard that he gave credit sometimes, but we assumed that his generosity was only extended to fine girls. I don't believe that he gave anyone anything. His wife would always be around somewhere making sure of that. Now, if we could catch that cute little daughter of his, we might have had a chance of at least getting a pop or some chips.

We were wrong as usual. It was so hard growing up with no extra money. Some people had a grandmother to go to but I didn't. Both of my grannies was dead. It was rough being a teenager. A lot of pressure trying to do the right thing. Unfortunately, there would be no pizza or bag full of goodies from the corner store for Tyrone and me that day.

I wanted to ask my mom for a few dollars but I overheard her telling my dad that we needed new shoes for school for both me and my sister. I couldn't bother her, plus I didn't want to hear the lecture on how much she gave up for me. "I could have been a great chef traveling all over the world, but no. I fell in love with your old daddy," she would say.

"I know," I would say back. "You said it a hundred times. Not long after, I popped out and you all had to get married."

I never understood why they had to get married just because she was pregnant. Didn't they want to get married? She always said they were young and they had no business having sex in the first place. It shamed our families and getting married made things more tolerable.

She liked when I asked questions. It was important to her that I understood the consequences of sex before I was old enough to know what I was doing. When it came down to girls she said, "Promise me you will save yourself for the right girl and get married first. Believe me, it would be much better for you. Take my word. Be careful." And, of course, I promised.

Tyrone was kind of in the same situation that I was in. He had a daddy at the time. His father married his mom when she was just a teenager, straight out of high school. All of the guys wanted her. She was beautiful on the outside, as well as the inside, not like some of those good-looking girls who put their noses in the air and turn their heads as though they didn't see you to keep from saying hello. How rude. Sometimes they didn't look that good anyway.

Now, Tyrone's father was not a very good-looking man but he knew how to talk to the ladies. He married Tyrone's mom before he went to the Military so that no one else could get to her.

He came back on leave and Tyrone was born. Every time he came home, she got pregnant. I think he did that also to make sure she was busy until he came home for good. When he came home for good he took a job as a truck driver. Of course, that kept him away from home too, like the Military. So, they were not used to seeing him that often anyway, although he took care of business.

He made sure they had everything they needed and sometimes he surprised them with things that they wanted. One day all of that changed when Tyron's father died in a serious accident in route to a trucking assignment.

They were devastated but had to go on without him, knowing that he had taken care of them all of these years. His mom just knew that he had insurance even though he never discussed any business with her. He would wire money to her to take care of things so she never questioned him. She figured they would be able to live decently for a while on his insurance before she would have to look for work.

This was far from the truth. She contacted his job's human resource office, asked about his insurance, and was told that a lawyer representing his family had already come by with his will to see what he had. She informed the gentleman that she was his wife and that he had three children. Tyrone's mother was totally confused since she had not solicited the services of a probate attorney to assist with her husband's affairs. Then it hit her like a ton of bricks. Her husband had another household... another wife... another family... The weight of the realization crushed her, the lies... the betrayal... the shame. She trusted him explicitly, never questioning and always trusting. Realizing the serious nature of the situation, and the devastation that he had caused, the HR rep gave her the contact information to the law firm representing the other family. He offered a quick apology and terminated the phone call. She contacted the lawyer, who told her that he could not give her the name of the lady, but that she needed to know that her husband had a family in Detroit. His insurance was left to that lady, his client, and her son. He was very sorry that she had to get that information from him like that. Her husband never mentioned a wife and family in Ohio.

His mom was devastated, of course. She trusted and depended on him for everything. This was a big blow to them. She had to get on government assistance, which she was ashamed to do. She had no other choice. She had some family in the city but they had their own problems. They couldn't help her. So, Tyrone tried his best to do what he could to help the family by cutting grass in the summer and shoveling snow in the winter. He did pretty good until now.

We were so afraid of going to jail, so we didn't steal, unlike Tyrone's brothers. They couldn't take what happened to them, so they turned to crime at an early age. They was so angry about what their father had done to the family they just didn't care anymore. It was very painful for their mom who now was going to school to be a nurse.

She told them things would get better but Tyrone was the only one who tried to do the right thing. As time went on, things did get better but money was always short and he understood that.

Our failure to bug Leroy to cough up a few dollars just to get us off his back did not work this time. He threw a curve ball at us. He would not come across the street where we were this time. "I'm out, guys. My dad is taking me out to lunch," he said. That was dirty of him. He knew our situation. How could he?

Both Tyrone and I said at the same time, "That rat is not my friend no more."

By now that was our reality. He didn't care about us anyway. We looked up and who came walking like he owned the city? Chuck, as we called him. Charlie Simpson: the ladies' man. Chuck was sixteen years old and had two baby mommas. Now get this… by older women. Can you believe it?

Now, no one was supposed to know this because he was underage, but he would brag about it. We didn't know if it was true or not but, if you saw the kids, you would swear up and down they were his. Chuck was a nice-looking man with fine hair like his father, but this time instead of him being in the DDC he was in the DMC: The Divorced Mom Club. Moms was just walking away from their homes and leaving their children. What a crazy time this was. That is how he got those babies, if they were his; He was looking for a momma figure. He had to grow up so fast. He was mature for his age.

Because he was sixteen he could work at the gas station or one of the baby mommas would give him something. He had to go to school though. His father would not allow him to drop out. He told him he had to graduate in order to get a better job.

He had the highest respect for his father; to take on two kids by himself, not knowing where his wife was, had to be hard and embarrassing. But he handled it. You never heard him complain. So, Chuck agreed that he should finish school.

"What up chumps? Where you going? I know you don't have bus fare," Chuck said.

"No, man. Waiting for you to throw a few dollars our way. I know you got paid," I said.

"Do I look like your daddy? I got a few dollars but not for you. Where you headed? I'm on my way to my girl's house now to see what I can get."

16

"What girl?"

"You know Felicia. We been kicking it for a while. She gives me anything I want."

"Yeah, I bet. You better watch out for those baby mommas while you kicking it with a girl your age for a change," I said. By the time Chuck got through running his mouth, I heard another voice.

"What yawl doing?"

No one said anything. We finished rapping with Chuck and he ran off into the store.

"What yawl doing?"

Again, this voice. We didn't notice anyone out but us. Tyrone walked away slowly. He said, "I'll see you later."

As he was walking away I said, "Wait, man, where you going? I'll go with you."

I had no idea where he was going but nothing was happening around here. My mom didn't teach me to be rude so I said, "We're just hanging out."

By then I glanced up a little to see this lady at the bus stop. I couldn't tell you what she looked like, all I saw was a big smile. Then she asked when school started. Tyrone looked back and his face said, "Man, this lady probably thinks we want to take something from her."

It was not impossible because young boys were robbing people at bus stops and stores. I said to the woman that I thought school would start in a couple of weeks, but I wasn't sure. Just when I said that and was about to catch up with Tyrone she said, "Here take this," and she mumbled something about "good boys" and put something in my hand.

I gladly took it, thinking maybe she heard us asking Chuck for money. She would give us a few dollars or maybe it was one of those prayer tracks that these people give out sometimes. I had a feeling it was a few dollars. I didn't care how much. I could get something. It felt like money but I wouldn't look at first. I called to Tyrone, "Wait up! This lady gave me something."

As I opened my hand it was more than enough cash for me, Tyrone, and Chuck to have a good time. We ran into the store and told Chuck what had happened. He ran out of the store to catch the lady, but she was already on the bus. "Man, she got on the bus already. I know you going to hook me up. How much you got?" Chuck asked. I showed him what I wanted him to see. I'm not a fool. I needed to hold on to some of this for another day.

By this time, Mr. Knuckles wanted to know what we was up to. As we lined the counter with all kinds of goodies he said, "Yawl know I don't do credit."

I whipped out some cash. "Who'd you steal that from?" he said. Now, he knew that stealing was not our way. He had seen us come in as kids and we never took anything.

I remember once some young boys, younger than us, robbed him. They had guns but he found out later that the guns were fake. He then put up some protection at the window for himself and his employees. "I'm just jiving with you. I know you didn't steal," he said. I told him about the lady at the bus stop and he too was surprised. Then he remembered that one time, a while back, some kids was buying candy and a lady told them to get what they wanted and she would pay for it.

I had not seen her in the store before; if she did come in, Mr. Knuckles would know. He knew almost everyone in the neighborhood. We knew that most of the people that lived in the hood was trying to make ends meet and having extra to give never happened. "She was on the bus so she could not have had too much but just felt sorry for you young men," Mr. Knuckles said. He never called us boys. "Did you get her name or remember what she looks like?"

"No, I didn't. I don't think I even said thank you or not. I was too glad to get this green," I said. Everything happened so fast. It was like, "I can't believe this," just when I was about to give up and go home. Me, Chuck, and Tyrone headed to the park. We had a good time eating and laughing but as I engaged with them I was glad my mom taught me respect.

I just did as she said. I loved my mother and had the highest respect for her after hearing how Chuck's mom just walked away from the family. Even though I listened to Mom, I did some devilish stuff. Nothing to get me locked up but my mom straightened me out, and not only with words.

She believed in one verse in the bible that she heard old folks say: Spare the rod, spoil the child. It had to be that verse as she put the rod to me, the child. I've seen kids hit their mothers and I couldn't believe it. I would always quote Momma's scripture when I see that.

The rest of our summer turned out pretty good. After that day we told Leroy about what he missed even though we knew he didn't care. He always had money. Well, it came closer and closer for school to start. I dreaded this. I was not good in English but I loved math. I could do without the other subjects but I did well enough to pass.

CHAPTER 2

SCHOOL'S IN

I hated going to my English class. I believe if the teacher was a female I could get with that. My mom said if I brought up my D grade in English this school year, I could have a party for my sixteenth birthday in December. I wanted the party but I knew I couldn't dig all those verbs and nouns that Mr. Sparks was teaching last year. It was foreign to me. Not having a party was no big deal. I would be satisfied just hanging out with the family.

Now Leroy, of course, was the man in school. His parents gave him a big lavish party for his fifteenth birthday. Just think what would happen on his sixteenth. His birthday just happened to fall in December also. I'd just go to his party and maybe Mom would buy me that black leather coat that I wanted if I just pass at all.

I met the boys on the corner like usual. Our school was in the neighborhood so we didn't have to walk that far. On the way to school we ran into your regular drunk, dope dealer, or sometimes people running out the deli because they stole something.

Where we lived was the pits but what could we do about it? Our families were doing the best they could. We had to deal with it and try to stay out of the gangs. That's why Chuck, Tyrone, Leroy, and me basically hung with each other to have each other's backs. Now, Leroy couldn't fight but he could talk a lot of game. The rest of us? Oh, we could get the job done if we had to, but we were lucky so far. No one bothered us too much.

I made my way through the halls of Cinnamon High. My first class was math which was great because I could do some numbers.

As I looked on my schedule I saw that English was fifth and Mr. Sparks name was not on it as my teacher. It said Lambkin. Was this a woman or a man? I didn't know because they only used last names. I asked Leroy if he had his English class yet and he said his was fifth period also.

We found out that Chuck also had his English in fifth period. Chuck was good in English, Tyrone was ok, and, like I said before, it was not my forte. I went to do what I had to do.

We had lunch third period. That worked out well for me. I can think better on a full stomach. When we went to class, I saw the most beautiful, tall sister. "Come on in. My name is Ms. Lambkin. I will be your English teacher this year. Mr. Sparks has moved to California for another teaching position. I have his notes as to where you guys are headed and what you need to work on," she said.

"I have each of your grades from last year and I do see that some of you can use some big help," she said as she glanced at me. "Now, lady, because you look good," I said to myself, of course, "don't point me out. I am not the only one in here who needs help."

How did she know anyway? She just got here and where did she come from? She said "Ms." I couldn't imagine a fine lady like that not married. Charlie Chan was not the only kid that like the ladies. I had my eye on a few honeys around. Maybe I'll be like Chuck and go for the older ones. Who knows? Right now, I had to get it together in this class.

Once I heard the kids talking about Leroy's party, something in me rose up and said, "OK, you be the man this year." Since Mr. Sparks was not there anymore, I now looked forward to fifth period, if only to daydream about Ms. Lambkin.

The first couple of months, things was not going so well in her class. I was still shooting my regular D's and sometimes a few F's on some of my papers. I could not get this thing together. When my mom asked how I was doing I would say about the same.

She never gave me a hard time about it and I know why. She had already told me what was going to happen if I did better, so it was up to me. Mom was so cool like that. She did my sister the same way. That made being a kid so much easier. I believe Leroy's parents put a lot of pressure on him to make good grades. He always seemed so uptight and stressed out. I knew his parents expected him to go to college. My mom just wanted me to finish high school at least to get some type of employment so that I would be able to support myself in the future. Who knew? I might get married and have a family.

I hung out with the boys after school. We loved to play basketball at the boys and girls club. That was, I believe, our saving grace during the winter months. When the recreation center closed for the winter, due to finance problems, Mom coughed up our fee for the Boys and Girls Club to keep us out of the streets.

They had computer classes, chess tables and lots of things that could keep you interested. I watched as the kids played chess. It seemed fascinating but it looked so hard. All I did was watch them and watch the honeys play this one girl Sabrina. She beat everybody. I was not the only one checking her out. Tyrone had his eyes on her too. He was my boy so I just let him have her.

I wasn't ready yet anyway. I concentrated on the chess game itself. It was October now and I was doing my usual in school. All of my classes, except English, was looking promising. It was almost report card time when Ms. Lambkin said, "OK I see that some of you are getting this class and some of you still need some help. We are going to try things a little different to see who catches on. I promise you, if you put your mind to it, everyone one of you can pass this class and go on to college if you desire."

She was a dreamer. Most of us in the class just wanted to make it to the next grade. College was not on my mind. Even though it would have been nice, this school thing was hard work.

I couldn't think of college right now. I was too young. I never thought to even look that far ahead. I was only in the eighth grade. Give me a break.

CHAPTER
3

THE ASSIGNMENT

"I want you to write a two-hundred-word essay about the most excited thing that happened to you in your life. This will count as eighty five percent of your first-quarter grade. This should bring some of you up if you work hard at it," Ms. Lambkin said.

I already knew the only exciting thing that happened to me was that lady this summer, so I knew I had this in the bag. Where to put those nouns and pronouns? I didn't know but I could write something.

She assigned the paper on a Thursday and we had until the following Thursday to complete the assignment. I was so glad she gave us some time. I thought she was going to say it would be due Monday. The weekend was approaching and I didn't want to waste my weekend on schoolwork.

I started working on my paper on Sunday after dinner. It had been a while since this happened and I did not want to forget anything about that day. It was important that I do a good job with this paper. I wanted to show Mom that I was trying hard. As I was writing, I was stuck on how to spell some big words I wanted to make this thing sizzle. All I knew was where to put a period. I called Chuck and Tyrone to see what they were writing. Neither one had a clue. "I can write about my new baby momma," Chuck said.

"Yeah right. They will put you out of school," I said. "For real though… you got a new baby momma?"

"No, man, I was just kidding you. I had some good things that happened. I don't tell you everything." Whatever it was, I knew it had to do with that basketball.

"I will make big money because I'm going to play basketball," Chuck said. Chuck was always dreaming. He was too easy to get upset to play basketball. I could see him knocking out the coach. That would be a disaster.

I finished writing and it sounded pretty good to me. "What you doing?" my mom hollered in my room. I went to the kitchen where she was and I showed her my paper.

"What's the assignment?" she asked.

"About the most excited thing that happened to me in my life," I said.

"Oh, all fifteen years of your life. What did you write about?" she asked. I told her the story about the lady at the bus stop.

"That's where you got the money from. One of our neighbors saw you and your friends in the store, called me and told me. I said nothing because I thought you would tell me. I was so afraid that one of you had taken the money from someone. I knew I didn't have any extra this summer. I was not concerned because you hadn't been in any trouble," she said.

"Let me see your paper," Mom said. After Mom read it, she began to help me put things into place and correct my spelling. I went back in and wrote it over then she said, "That's it you got it now."

I told her how it was going to bring my grade up if I do a great job. "I think you will. I wish you had told me about the lady this summer. I could have used some of that money you had," she said and we laughed. My paper was done that night. I remembered I had homework due in math on Monday, so I had to get it done before bed time.

My mom made sure we got eight hours of sleep and breakfast before we went to school. I was glad that sometimes Tyrone would come over for breakfast. My mom could cook but his mom was not that great in the kitchen.

Monday while in class, this girl named Courtney (I think she had a crush on me) wanted to know what my paper was about. I knew she was just picking at me. "None of your business," I said.

"You can't write about something that never happened. You're not a nice person so nothing exciting will ever happen for you," Courtney said.

Little did she know I was nice. I just didn't like her. She was kind of cute but too chubby for me. Not that I'm judging. I used to have some chubbiness on me from Mom's cakes and pies, but I was too handsome to be chubby. If she wasn't so annoying I could look beyond her big mouth. I probably would take a second look.

We went to the boys and girls club after school. Everyone was gathered around the chess table. A chess challenge was going on between that girl and two boys. She whipped them good. With all eyes on the chess match, that left the computer stations free. I knew a little about the computer, like turning it on and opening up a file. My sister showed me that much.

Typing my paper would not only surprise my teacher that I could think that far, it just might help me get a decent grade so that I could have my sweet sixteen party. I was able to type my paper. I knew I was going to get a good grade, at least a C. Then I could have my party.

Now, Ms. Lambkin asked on Tuesday, "How many of you have started on your assignment?" I was always the last one to raise my hand for anything in this class. When Mr. Sparks would say, "Mr. Rome, do you have anything to add to the class?" his voice was so annoying that it made my ears burn. He took more time with most of the other students in the class. When it came to me, it was as if I was invisible. He never took the time to explain anything.

I didn't raise my hand because the question didn't apply to me. The majority of the class raised their hands. "OK, that's a good start. Remember, the rest of you, you will only have one day left and think about your grade," she said. I then raised my hand. "Yes Mr. Rome?"

"You didn't ask who finished their papers."

"I'm sorry. Raise your hand if you finished your paper."

I proudly raised my hand along with Ms. Thing Courtney. She had her faults but the girl was smart and always had her stuff together.

I was excited. Usually Courtney would be the only one in the class that had her assignments done in advance. Now she had some competition. "Good I'll see you guys tomorrow," said Ms. Lambkin. I caught up with Leroy who said, "I know you didn't do your paper." I am sure that is what Leroy was hoping, due to my past reputation. He heard talk about my birthday party this year if I could get my grades up. He had some competition. Everyone would be at his party but they would rather come to mine if I had one... "I did do my paper. Did you do yours?" I said.

"I finished mine too." Leroy saw that I was serious about having this party. I kicked it around a bit with the fellows before I went home. I had only one assignment to do for math, so I had a nice easy night. I took my shower and went to bed earlier than usual.

"Are you feeling OK, Rome," Mom said. "You are going in early tonight."

She knew that was not like me. Tyrone came over most nights to hang out. "I'm doing OK," I said. "Tyrone did not call so he is probably busy. I just don't have anything to do right now."

"Oh, you have something to do," Mom said. "What about the garage? You know I need to get my car in there before the winter."

"You're right, Mom. I'll get it. I will," I said. Why was she nagging at me? This wasn't like her. Then I thought it was probably my dad doing something silly like he always did. I would not dare talk back. She had a good back hand and she was good at using it if she had to. Maybe she'll tell me about it tomorrow. In the meantime, I would get that garage cleaned soon.

I woke up like usual. Mom had our breakfast ready but she didn't look so well. I hoped she wasn't ill. That was the next big thing happening in two thousand ten. You would hear of people dying every day from diseases we never heard of. I don't know what I would do without my mother. Besides my dad, me and my sister had no other family. Mom was an only child and her parents had already passed away.

"Mom, are you alright? You don't look so happy this morning. What did dad do?" I asked. I was careful with my words with her because I had never seen her like this before, so something had to be awfully wrong. It's kind of funny to me now that I think about it. Mom was always asking us if we were alright. Now we have to check on her which I never thought about. She was the mom. I was the child. How selfish is that?

She grabbed a cup of coffee and sat next to my sister. "My job at the hospital is over," she said. "They had to downsize and the part-time people went first. I don't know what will happen or if we will be able to keep the house or not. Maybe your dad will help out more."

I was so relieved that she wasn't going to die that it didn't matter to me if we were in a tent, as long as we were together. I hugged her. "Mom, I'll be sixteen soon," I said. "I'll get a job and help out."

"That means you won't be able to have your party... and you worked so hard on that paper."

"It's OK, Mom. I'll have one next year. I probably won't pass English this year anyway. Even if I get a good grade on my paper, what about the rest of the year?"

"Do your best, OK?" She kissed me on the cheek as she walked away, trying to hold back the tears so we would not see her cry.

I was a bit upset about not being able to show Leroy who the man was this time. I'll get him next year. I know Mom still wanted me to do better in school, so I made up my mind to keep trying. Who knows? Maybe one day I could pay for my own party. Thursday came and I didn't say anything more about a party. I hoped no one would ask me about it. When we got to our English class, Ms. Lambkin asked again who all had their assignments. This time everyone raised their hands. Then she threw a curve ball at us. For me anyway. If the others were prepared for this, I wasn't.

She called on Leroy to read his paper before the class. She knew that she called the right one first. He loved to be up front and being first is icing on the cake for him. Leroy read about the trip that his father took him on in the Rocky Mountains, just the two of them, hiking, catching fish and just having some father and son time, and this coyote that would not go away but he was a friendly coyote Leroy said.

Yea right. I don't believe anything that he says. He has such an imagination. I'm sure he could write a book on his adventures.

Everyone knew him and his stories and I'm sure, like me, they were glad when his paper ended. "Nice job," Ms. Lambkin said to him then she called on the next student. I was glad it wasn't me. I wanted to be last to see the reaction that the class had for each person. This class was brutal to some of the students.

But Ms. Lambkin would not let them go too far. She did welcome some clean laughter when one student paper was about her meeting the President when she went to Washington to see the White House with her family. She was walking down the hall when the President came up to her and asked her name and what did she plan on doing when she graduated. She was so nervous that she puked on the president. We didn't believe that.

It was getting down to the wire. So far, no one had anything exciting to tell and that made me a little more comfortable to get up front and do what I do.

My anxiety kicked in. Oh no… I hated getting in front of people. Mom couldn't afford to get my teeth fixed and I was a bit ashamed. This was it. I just would not make the grade. I'll settle for whatever I get. After Leroy, she called on the next student. Before that student went, I raised my hand and asked if we all had to read our papers in front of the class. "Yes," that is part of your grade too," Ms. Lambkin said.

As each name was called, I think Ms. Lambkin noticed my anxiety and probably would save me for last. Good. That would give me time to get myself together. As I calmed down a bit, it was Courtney's time to read her paper. I believe she made the stuff up. She was talking about learning to fly an airplane. Who would let a fifteen-year-old learn how to fly? The class was eating it up. They laughed when she said she almost wet her pants.

When she was done, the bell rang. "These are some great essays and I think we should use tomorrow to discuss what we have heard so far. The rest of you should be prepared to read yours on

Monday," Ms. Lambkin said. I was saved for real by the bell and a few more days. How sweet. I had time to work on my nerves. I was a good-looking boy, so I thought anyway. Just never felt comfortable talking in a crowd.

Tyrone and two other students hadn't read their papers yet, so I felt better. Tyrone was just as bad as I was. He was kind of quiet and to put him in front of people would be a disaster. I hoped he would be first on Monday. I don't know what he wrote about. We were always together and this was the only exciting thing that happened to us.

I asked Tyrone what he was writing about and he agreed that nothing exciting happened to him. "Nothing but bad things. My pops doing what he did and leaving us in this situation. I'm not old enough to get a job, which is frustrating. We could get on food stamps, which my momma just hates. She doesn't want to depend on the county. But we have no choice."

I felt so bad for Tyrone. He was right; he had a rough summer. The only time that he was able to laugh for little was that day. He had a little crush on my sister but she was too old for him. Plus, she didn't give him the time of day.

We were both about to turn sixteen and would be able to get a job at the recreation center, so that was some kind of hope. I tried to cheer him up but I had my own problems getting through this year to graduate and to try to do something with my life.

I told him to come over to the house for dinner. "I am sure Mom is cooking something good and I will help you with your paper," I said. I could tell that made him feel a little better, especially the part about dinner he could eat.

Even though I didn't ask Mom in advance, she knew what his family was going through and she would make room for him. It was the weekend too. We had movie night on Friday nights, so he would fit in around the TV just like family.

Tyrone was my only friend. I would give my life for him and I think he would do the same for me. But how many people can say that? He did as he said. Mom had no problem with him. She was glad to see him. After a dinner of red beans, rice and baked chicken, which was delicious as always, she made some chocolate chip cookies.

We watched some movies then Tyrone asked if he could spend the night since it was getting late and we had not touched the paper. It was OK with Mom as long as he called his mom to let her know.

The next day, we told my mom that I was trying to help Tyrone with his paper and we didn't know what to write about. Mom told Tyrone that it would be a good idea to write about his experiences at home. "You could tell them how scary it was at first and then about how you stepped up to the plate, and how proud your mom was of you. Your fear turned into excitement when you looked back and saw how well things were going for your family," she said.

Tyrone and I went to work and came up with something that would get him at least a passing grade. We looked in my closet and found a red shirt for me and a blue shirt for Tyrone. I told him at least we would look good. My mom had bought me that red shirt a month ago but I wouldn't wear it. "Men do not wear red," I told her when she gave it to me.

My mom knew my fears of facing the class, so she showed me and Tyrone what to do to get over the fear. She had us laughing about how to imagine the students was a piece of chicken looking so delicious it will make you smile. I put the shirt on with some black pants and I knew I had it going on. I'd look so sharp they would just check me out. When it was time for class, I was still a little nervous but I looked in the bathroom mirror one last time.

The students who had already read their papers were waiting. They knew that when Mr. Sparks was teaching, he would not call on me that often. Tyrone was looking good and when he read his paper it was very well received. The class felt sorry for him, knowing what he went through, but was proud of him for helping his family through those bad times.

She called on one of the other students to read their paper, and then it was my time. I was the last student, which was good. Then Ms. Lambkin called me. I did what my mom said and added some humor. I told them I thought the lady was a cougar digging on me and some more stuff.

When I finished, the entire class laughed and clapped. I was the only one who received that much attention. I figured a good grade was definitely in store for me. Then someone asked if I had seen her again? Before I could answer, someone else asked if I had been back to the bus stop? "OK, class," Ms. Lambkin cut in. "One at a time. Before the bell rings, ask your questions."

Courtney said, "She was just feeling sorry for you. She didn't want you. Nobody wants you."

"OK, Courtney, that's enough. Good job, class. See you tomorrow. I will try my best to have your papers graded for tomorrow."

I had no homework for a change. This was good. I could relax and play some basketball with the guys. Before Mom could ask, I told her what happened in class when I read my paper. "I know you will get a good grade. I am sorry about your party," she said. It was OK. I felt like the man anyway.

I met Tyrone at the basketball court. "Man, thank you for helping me out. That was cool but not for me. I don't like getting in front of people. I guess you'll have that big party now. You know, Leroy is sending out his invites to the whole school, it seems like," He said.

"No sweat. My mom got cut from one of her jobs. We can't swing the party this time."

That afternoon was sweet. We just happened to have some good weather and I found myself cleaning out the garage like I told Mom I would do a long time ago.

She was very happy to see it. "It's about time," she said, then she gave me the biggest kiss on my cheek, something she did not do that often but, when she did, it made me feel closer to her.

I thought about my paper and was looking forward to seeing what grade I would get. Even though my plans had changed I still wanted to get a good grade. Tuesday came soon enough. As the bell rang for fifth period, my heart now began to pound. I was a bit eager for the first time to get to class.

Everyone sat in anticipation as Ms. Lambkin handed us our papers. There was so much noise as each student called out their grade, some with excitement and some with OK. I took my paper and saw a B plus. "That's what I'm talking about!" I said out loud.

The first time in this class I had something to be proud of. Ms. Lambkin explained the grading of the papers and that everyone in the class had passed that quarter because of their essays.

"Now, class, I am so proud of all of you, but some of you exceeded my expectations. You used great grammar and had punctuation in the correct place. That is what the essay writing was all about. I wanted to see how much you learned over the years and, I must say, things are not as bad as I thought," said Ms. Lambkin, "Here is a thought that I had: Since this class was so excited about Mr. Rome's essay, why don't we use it as a class project for the rest of the semester? We can come up with ideas on how we can reach out and find this lady, things like the school newspaper, the Internet, I know everyone has Facebook. What do you think?"

Man, was my chest puffed out. I did this. I made this happen. Everyone was on board. Courtney said, "We need a name for our project."

"Well, Mr. Rome, since it is your paper what do you think?" asked Ms. Lambkin.

"How about 'Heaven Must Be Missing an Angel: I saw her at the Bus Stop?'"

"It sounds good."

Ideas came from all over the room as to how we can approach this. First, we would write a letter in the school paper, after we ask the principal. Nowadays, you have to be so careful. People will sue you for anything.

We decided to distribute the school paper in the neighborhood. So, I'm sure if this happened to anyone else, they might come forward and/or the person might come forward. We didn't know what would happen but we were so excited.

It was time to move on to the next class when Chuck caught up with me. "So, I guess you're the big man on campus now with the paper buzz," he said.

"You got it. What I didn't hear is what you got on your paper talking about your new girl. You are a joke, man. You need to get serious. By the time you finish high school you will have so many baby mommas."

"You're just jealous. Where's your girl?"

This got me to thinking. I didn't have any girls on my radar at this time. Ms. Lambkin looked like the kind of woman I would want. She dressed well, always had a smile and she was fine too. But I knew I couldn't go there. Maybe when I graduated I would check her out.

Ms. Lambkin told Mrs. Crowley about our project that we wanted to run in the school paper and how this all came about. She was surprised to hear that I was one of the students not likely to succeed, according to Mr. Sparks, and how my paper started this. She was glad to hear it.

"I'll come by your classroom tomorrow and discuss how we will do this. You made a break through with this. young man," Said Mrs. Crowley

"Oh, you should see the other students' excitement and how hard they are working and bringing their grades up in this class and some of their other classes from what I hear from the teachers," said Ms. Lambkin proudly.

Mrs. Crowley did as she said; she came to Ms. Lambkin's fifth period class. "Well, class," she said. "I will give you all two months to run your letter in the school paper. After that time, we will see if we need more time or not. Is that agreed with the class?"

"Yes, that is not a problem," Ms. Lambkin said.

I didn't feel that a couple of months would be long enough but I had to go along with it. "Now, before you take it to the printer, I need to read what is going to be printed," Mrs. Crowley said.

"OK, class, this is our go ahead. We can work on the letter tomorrow. Get a good night sleep tonight because we will be rolling for a while, we hope. I do expect you to keep up with your other classes. I don't want to hear that you are goofing off or I will cut this project, OK?" Ms. Lambkin said.

Mom was glad to see how I was doing with my attitude about school. She saw that I liked school now. That Thursday night was a parent-teacher conference. I took my letter home to Mom; she was looking forward to going because, for once, there was some good news about me and not what Mr. Sparks said about my needing to be in a slower class. It was difficult to keep up with the class. I couldn't understand when to use a noun or pronouns or anything that Mr. Sparks was trying to teach us. I just didn't like his vibe and so I think I didn't try hard enough.

My mom wanted Mr. Sparks to challenge me more instead of allowing me to turn in papers that were not up to par. She wanted him to challenge me because she knew I could do better.

When she came back from the teacher parent conference she said how all of my teachers were so proud of my work. She was glad to finally meet Ms. Lambkin, and she understood why I talked about her so much. "She is a nice teacher," she said.

The next day was the day to get the letter together for the school paper to see what would happen. I became a little nervous.

You hear on the news and in the paper about people doing good things for people all the time. So, why was I so hyped about this?

I guess because no one had ever done anything for me except my mom and dad (when he could). Maybe someone else was out there and this lady did something for them that changed their lives. It was worth looking into even if I was laughed at.

It was worth it to me to move on. Plus, I was making better grades in my English class.

CHAPTER 4

THE LETTER GOES TO PRESS

The letter was put in the school paper and it read as follows:

> *The 501 English class at Cinnamon High School is looking for a lady that we call our "Bus Stop Angel" on June 12th, 2010. Around 12:30 p.m. a nice lady gave a couple of young boys some money and we didn't get to say thank you.*
>
> *At the time, we had no idea someone would be nice to us. This person stepped up to the plate and changed our lives. Never before, or since then, has anything like that happened to myself or any of the guys I was with that day. If anyone reading this article knows of anyone that has done such a thing, please contact us. We do not believe that this was a coincidence. w\We are in the middle of a class project to contact this person and show her the appreciation that she deserves. You can e-mail us at 501@ cinnamonhigh.com or write to:*
>
> *The Bus Stop Angel*
> *Cinnamon High School*
> *3262 East Prosperity Dr.*
> *Cleveland, Ohio 44129*
> *C/O English 501*

The letter went to print that day, and then was distributed in the neighborhood. As time went on, I began to fall in love with school and writing. I think I found my thing. Tyrone and Chuck were good at basketball and they were hoping to get in college on a scholarship. But me? I didn't like the game that much. I only kicked around with the guys. We were learning so much in English that Ms. Lambkin gave us a classroom party. It was awesome. Her other classes began to get jealous and felt that she was not being fair to them. Well if they worked hard like 501, then they could have had a party too.

It took a while but her other classes began to do well. The principal was very pleased. At our quarterly assembly Ms. Lambkin received a plaque for her dedication to her classes. They also surprised our class with a ribbon to display on our board for outstanding progress. Now the entire class was pumped up. For once we were headed in the right direction. Up and up was the only way I wanted to go from now on. It's funny how one small thing can change your whole life.

For weeks, we didn't receive any correspondence to our letter in the school paper. I began to get a little discouraged. Ms. Lambkin noticed it. She said, "You worked hard, and we might not get any letters, but you changed the atmosphere of the school. From what I understand, Mr. Sparks had you down as a jokester but you showed up for class every day, so he gave you that D for that. If he could see you now…"

If she only knew what she had done to my ego and if I was old enough I would ask her to marry me. When I graduated, of course. She knew how to make me feel special, just like my mom.

I never thought about going to college before but it was a possibility now. I began to admire Ms. Lambkin more and more. I guess you can say I had a schoolboy crush but that was it. After not hearing anything for a while, and the deadline that Mrs. Crowley had given us was approaching, Ms. Lambkin asked the principal if we could let the letter stay a little longer. She agreed since we were doing so well. Cinnamon High had become one of the conversations in the neighborhood. Students that didn't care about school were now taking it more seriously and were beginning to bring their grade point average up. The school itself had made great progress to get a grant for new classrooms since the students were doing so well. This time we printed more than the first time. Courtney said, "Let's post them at all of the bus stops in the neighborhood." That was a good idea.

Every day I would go to the mail room looking for letters. They were tired of seeing me coming. "If we get something for you I will run to your class OK?" they said. I was anxious. I forgot all about Leroy's party and no one asked me about mine. The word was out that my party was cancelled. In the past, I would have been ashamed to face up to my friends when I said things and they didn't happen, but this time it didn't matter. I guess I was growing up. About to be sixteen and finally thinking about my future. Not bad.

Have you ever had the feeling like something was about to happen and you wish you knew what it was so that you could prepare yourself? As I got dressed for school that morning, I decided to wear the red shirt my mom had bought me a while back. That red grew on me. I liked it better this time. Mom would be glad to see me with it on again.

When I went down for breakfast, Mom was cooking something. Her back was turned and my sister said, "Mom, Rome got on the red shirt."

As Mom turned around, she said, "You look so handsome. Thank you for wearing the shirt again. You look so handsome."

It didn't take much for me to blush when Mom called me handsome.

I met up with the guys to see what was happening with them. It seemed that Tyrone's mom had landed a really good job at a college in the Health Department. Good for them. Now I could go over his house and pig out sometimes. Chuck was doing what he do but seemed to be taking life a little bit more serious than before. He probably realized having all of those baby mommas was not a good idea at such a young age anyway.

Now, we had not seen Leroy except in class. He seemed to have pulled away from us. He wasn't in the spotlight anymore. He thought nothing good was ever going to happen to anyone but him. How wrong he was. We heard through the grapevine that he cancelled his party. He gave some lame excuse about his mom and dad taking him on a cruise. Still trying to be in the spotlight. I knew my mom couldn't afford to take me on a cruise. If Leroy's family had it like that, good for him. "Here we go again," Chuck said. "He's at it again. Just got to be the man."

It didn't matter to me anymore I had other things on my mind. For the first time, I too had dreams and there were possibilities. We stopped by the corner store to shoot the breeze with Mr. Knuckles. "I read in the paper about your school project. You know there was a lady in the store a while back. One of the kids didn't have enough money to buy something. She stepped right in and told all three of the kids to get what they wanted and they did. I bet she's the lady but she left before I could say anything to her.," he said.

I couldn't wait to get to class and tell Ms. Lambkin. I told her what Mr. Knuckles had said and how I forgot to mention it before. This gave us the exhilaration to move on. We shared the information with the class and excitement came back to the room. Now there was more hope that someone might contact us if this lady was still around. Before class could start the editor of the school paper herself came in the class with a red envelope. She handed it to Ms. Lambkin and said, "This is what you guys have been waiting for. I took the privilege of bringing it to you myself. Now, what do I get?"

We applauded her and she laughed as she walked out of the door. "OK, class, here it is," Ms. Lambkin said. "Mr. Rome, would you like to do the honors of reading it to the class?"

This time I had no problem facing the class. Plus, today I was looking exceptionally handsome. Everyone was quiet, anticipating what was said in the letter. All eyes were on me. Even Ms. Lambkin sat in the front row and not at her desk this time. Now I saw those big, beautiful legs which made it hard for me to concentrate, but I had to get it together. It read:

Dear English 501,

As I was having coffee this morning, my neighbor brought me this flyer from the bus stop down the street. I used to take it some years ago. My eyesight is not as good as it used to be, so my neighbor read it to me. Four years ago, I told her about the young lady at the bus stop who gave me her coat. So, here is my story. I hope that you can read it OK. It's important to me to write it myself. I had an experience with a lady at the bus stop about four years ago.

I found myself alone when I was having some major pain on one of my teeth at age seventy-five. I was blessed to still have teeth, I'm sure some of you are saying to yourself. I called the dental school and was told that I could come that morning. My problem then was how I would get there.

My son was out of town, the bus system that would pick me up had to be called two days in advance, and I was hurting. I knew the city bus picked up down the street but I wasn't sure if it took me to the dental school or not. I was hurting so bad that I had to take my chances. I could ask the bus driver.

I hurried and got dressed. The sun was shining. I didn't think I needed a heavy jacket, so I put on my spring jacket and rushed out the door. As I stepped outside I realized I made a mistake. It was a bit brisk out but I was afraid I would miss the bus. I thought maybe it would be there soon, so I walked as fast as these old legs could take me.

To make a long story short, as I approached the bus stop this big smile met me. This lady was the only one at the bus stop. We exchanged "good mornings." She saw I was nervous, old white woman who was taught to not trust people of color. There I was needing help from whomever would help me at the time.

She smiled and that was a good sign to me that I could trust her. I was too afraid to ask her where the bus was going when she asked me where were I going. "Not to be nosy," she said. I was glad she was nosy. I told her and asked if this bus would take me. She said, "Yes." How relieved I was.

Before we could finish talking she said, "There is the bus now." She allowed me to get on first. What manners she was taught by someone. As I sat down I made sure I sat in a place where a space was left for her, hoping she would sit with me. She did. I know that she felt my body shivering. It was colder than I thought. I didn't say much because I was in pain and I hoped she didn't think I was being rude. "I can get off of the bus stop by the dental school," she said. "Don't worry. I'll show you where to get off."

Now I could relax a little. When we approached the bus stop she said, "This is it." We both got off the bus and she did the most unselfish thing that had ever happened to me. She took off her coat *and gave it to me. It was a beauty. "Oh no, I can't take your coat," I said. "It's cold out here."*

"I'll be fine," she said as she walked me to the dental school and made sure I was signed in. I began to take the coat off to give her. "No, you keep it. You will need it to get back home.," she said. I didn't feel the pain in my mouth anymore I felt warmth in my heart along with my body.

If this is the young lady and you find her, please let her know how grateful I was and still am to this day. I still have and cherish her beautiful coat. I was hoping before I leave this earth I would be able to say thank you to that young lady again. I shared this story with my son and others.

I looked up from reading to tears all over the room. Even Chuck was fighting back tears because he was too manly to let anyone see him cry. It was time for the class to end when Ms. Lambkin was able to get herself together and say, "Well, class, we can believe that this person might have touched more lives. I will share this letter with the principal and we will see if we have more letters coming. By the way, you all are working so hard. Did you notice in this lady's letter how she used her vocabulary and punctuation marks? It seems that she might have been an English teacher herself. Who knows?"

Excited about what was happening, I focused on my schoolwork. While I was concentrating on school, my mom was secretly preparing a birthday party after all. She was so proud of me and how I turned my grades around in all of my classes. Tyrone was in charge of telling the students about the party and that it was a secret.

My mom rented the party center and I had the best sixteenth birthday ever. I don't know how she did it she wouldn't tell me. I was happy that it was the talk of the school for a long time.

Time had passed and no more letters, so we took that as that was it and we were satisfied. I was learning so much in class. I couldn't believe that it was me. I now knew what I wanted to do with my life. I wanted to write stories.

Ms. Lambkin always seemed to read my mind. One day in class she did it to us again. We had to face the class and say what we wanted to do with our lives and why. This time I was glad to be number one to raise my hand because I knew for sure I wanted to write, which was no surprise to her.

CHAPTER
5

THE MAILBAG

Several months after all the excitement of my birthday had calmed down, I felt like a young man now. The editor of the paper came into class with a mail bag, smiling. "I believe you all are looking for this," she said. Time had passed, so we thought that one letter was probably all we would get and did not expect to get any more.

We were overjoyed. "OK, class, I know this is exciting but we have to tone it down," Ms. Lambkin said as she opened the mailbag. Inside there were many letters. White envelopes, red envelopes, blue envelopes, so many different colors, and some of them was thick.

The letters were addressed to our class. At last! What we had hoped would happen did happen and, wow, it was cool. We thanked the editor for bringing them in and she told us how excited she was for us.

This time, Ms. Lambkin asked Courtney to pick a letter out of the bag and read it to the class. She gladly did. The whole while she doubted my story from the beginning, but went along with the class. Now she was on board. There were several letters as each person read before the bell rang. Some of the letters were funny and some were sad but they all had something in common. Our assignment for the next day was to continue reading and talking about what each person had to say.

In class the next day everyone was really pumped up. It seemed as if everyone was ready to contribute to the class. We read more and more. Some of the letters were long and some just a few lines of what happened to them with a stranger, maybe this stranger. We read on until the bell rang. We had just a few more to read the next day. At the end of the reading Ms. Lambkin asked, "Who can tell me what each person in these letters has in common with each other?"

Hands were raised and answers were blurted out with so much enthusiasm. Something was happening in the class and it was good. Some of us had the same answers and they were all correct: The lady knew their needs, her smile, and her not wanting anything in return.

"But how did she know?" someone asked. That started me to thinking again about something that my mom told me a long time ago. We did not attend Church on a regular basis but Mom believed that there was a higher power and she also believed in angels.

"Angels comes in all forms and all colors," she said to me one day. "And you will know when you are approached by one." This is what she believed. I too am with her on that now. Looking back on that day, we had a need and this lady stepped in right on time. More letters came in for a couple of weeks. It was the buzz of the school.

The search to find this person was now personal. My life was taking a turn for the better. I was old enough now to get a part-time job after school to help my mom.

Pretty soon the letters stopped but we had enough to know that this was no ordinary person. She was special and hopefully one day we would find her, she would reveal herself, or someone would know who she was.

I excelled in school. Ms. Lambkin allowed me to hold on to the letters just in case I wanted to pursue this further one day. I was so grateful to her for allowing me to take this as far as it went.

I promised her that I would not let it go. I would continue to search for this lady who changed my life for the better. Not only my life but it put Cinnamon High School in the public eye. We were doing things now and students were succeeding and reaching for better futures for the first time in a long time.

Being an inspiration to the students made me feel good. I felt like I was being respected for my smarts for a change and I did not want to lose that feeling. My mom was so proud. My sister stopped hanging with the girls that she called her "friends." They were getting her in trouble. She also wanted to make Mom proud of her. She went to beauty school and became a beautician. Mom is helping her get her own shop.

My sister and I just wanted to live a decent life. We didn't talk about dreams for our future because, after dad left, we only had Mom to depend on and she was doing her best. We knew why Mom never gave up on us and never put pressure on us. She always said, "Do your best. That is all I ask of you." Mom was feeling good about us as a family and she wanted to let my dad know that we were going to be OK.

She called my dad and asked if he could come to dinner on Sunday, bringing his new family. It was time for us to let the past go and look out for each other. He must have said yes because she handed me the phone. After we talked he asked to speak with my sister, something he had not done in a long time.

It was good to hear his voice again. I could tell he was glad to hear from Mom and to talk to us. That Sunday we had a wonderful time with no arguing. I told him about my writing and what I wanted to do with my life and my sister told him about herself and what she was up to.

You could tell he was proud. His new wife and children fit right in with us and we promised to get together more regularly.

Before he left, he gave my mom an envelope. In it was enough money to help us finance some things that we wanted for a change instead of just our needs.

Graduation day came and I graduated in the top twenty of the school. I was proud. My dad and his family were there. I received an award for being an inspiration to the school and turning my D grades into A's and B's.

Everyone cheered. Wow, I was on cloud nine. My mom had used the money from my dad to take care of my dental problems. I looked good and I smiled big. It was my moment in life, which I thought would never happen.

After the ceremony, Mr. Sparks came to congratulate me and give me a package. I was surprised that he remembered me. I anxiously opened the beautiful wrapped package. Inside was the most beautiful, brown briefcase with my name engraved on the front. I thanked him and we shook hands as he said, "I am so proud of you. I see that you could learn and that I was wrong."

Of course, we went out to eat and made sure that Ms. Lambkin was with us. She made all this possible. She stepped out of the box and gave us who were called "losers" hope. All her classes became a success over the years and her students ended up in great colleges, living out their dreams.

If you walked in Cinnamon High today, you would see a picture of her and a plaque for a teacher who took a leap.

CHAPTER
6

MY DREAM JOB

I didn't make any college plans out of town. Being a momma's boy, I took some courses in journalism at the community college. I really wanted to see if this was what I had a passion for. I wrote my first novel about my summer experience. It was published right before I graduated. I was proud that the book was published. I wasn't expecting it to be a best seller, but it was doing well in the bookstores. That alone made me proud.

My mom got her copy before anyone else, of course. "This is good," she said. I took copies to the high school where everything got started. While I was deciding on what to do with my life next, my instructor told me about a position as an editor with the New York Rising Stars. She thought I was that good and said she would put in a recommendation for me.

It was amazing how things were working out. Even though I didn't want to leave my mother and sister I knew I had to take this opportunity if it was presented to me. I sent my resume to the head of the New York Rising Stars then I told my mother about it.

She was, as expected, sad that I would not be around to pester her (as she says) but happy for me. As I anticipated hearing about the job, I found out that Ms. Lambkin had taken a teaching position in California. I definitely had to let her know what was happening in my life because she played a big part.

I received a letter stating that I was accepted for the job. I made arrangements to stay with a friend in New York while I looked for an apartment. Before I left town, the fellows and I got together and wished each other the best. We promised to stay in touch with each other.

Would you believe it the only person that didn't go to college was the very person we thought that would? Leroy Jackson. He ended up getting a girl pregnant and marrying her. His parents were OK with it. They wanted grandchildren. They would be well taken care of.

As I worked hard with my company moving up the ranks was like a roller coaster. It seemed that I was an asset to the company. I was so busy working and making money that I never stopped to look into my love life. I didn't have to. Mom did it for me. She was always trying to set me up on a blind date with somebody's daughter that lived in Ohio. She was always asking when she was going to get some grand babies. I didn't have anyone special. I dated a few times but nothing to write home about.

I was looking for someone who had the smile that I remembered and seemed as though so many others remembered. I was thinking, if I found her, maybe she had a daughter. You know what they say: like mother, like daughter. That would be another story.

I wondered about Ms. Lambkin. Out of all of those years, I knew nothing about her family life. Was she ever married and did she have any kids? It's crazy now that I think about it. She never talked about herself. She was always at school for us anytime we needed her.

I called the school one day to get her contact information but I understood that they could not give that information out without the person's permission. I told the secretary who I was and asked if I could leave my number to have her contact me. "I know who you are Mr. Rome. This is Courtney. I was in English 501 with you," the secretary said.

"How are you? I thought you went to school to be a nurse."

"I did. Now I am the school nurse here and secretary when the regular girl is out."

"That's great!"

"I heard you were moving up the ladder in New York, Mr. Rome. Your name is still the talk of the school. When are you coming to visit us?"

"I don't know right now. It might be soon. That's why I want to contact Ms. Lambkin. I want to see how she is doing and if she plans to visit Cleveland any time in the near future."

"OK, I have to follow the rules. So, I will contact her and give her your number. It was so good talking to you. When you're in town, don't forget to come by and see me. I still live with my mom."

"What no babies or baby daddy?"

"Not me. I haven't found the right one yet. How about you?"

"Nothing got me. I'm still searching for the right one."

Courtney did as she promised. Within a couple of days Ms. Lambkin called me. We talked for hours about everything that was happening in our lives. She didn't talk much about her personal life. She was still doing some teaching in which I was glad to hear for she was a good teacher. She never spoke about having anyone in her life or not. I wanted to ask but I didn't want to make her uncomfortable. Maybe one day she would share with me but not now.

Before we hung up the phone she asked if I thought of pursuing the story that I had written previously about the missing angel. I thought about it I said that meant I would have to go back to Cleveland for a while. "Maybe I will someday," I said.

Little did I know that someday would be sooner than I thought. Mom called to ask me if I knew that my book was selling like wildfire in Cleveland. I had no idea. I left all that in my mother's hands. I didn't have much time to discuss the book sales with her.

I had no idea things were going so well. The last time Mom and I talked about the book, she said that it was doing well and that the people we knew were buying it. Of course, the faculty at Cinnamon High School were also purchasing it.

"What brought this about?" I thought.

"It seems that someone wrote to the newspaper that she believed that she knew who you might be looking for. The paper ran another story on your book."

Now I knew I had to go home. I asked Mom to set up a book signing, if possible, at my old high school. I thought that would be the perfect place to do that.

Mom did just that and it was scheduled for the following weekend, which was no problem. I hadn't used any of my vacation days since I had my job. My boss said it was no problem just as long as I came back.

"I will be back. I love what I do. Anyway, the book won't make me rich. It will be enough to get the money back that I put in, I hope. And help mom with whatever her needs are," I said.

Now I had this great job and the book seemed like it was going to be a success. I still felt empty inside. Something was missing. I needed someone to share all of this with but I just didn't want any drama. I heard that Leroy and his wife had lots of drama in their marriage where she left home for a while but his parents convinced her to come back. I know that relationships have ups and downs but I want to find someone that we can have more ups than downs. That's not too much to ask. I was a bit older and wiser. I was determined not to be like my father.

My flight got into the airport in Cleveland with just enough time for me to get a rental and get to the school. The food on the plane wasn't great but I ate just enough to keep my stomach from talking for me while at the book signing. I would take Mom out to dinner when things were over. When I got to the school the parking lot was full. Maybe they were having a meeting at the school also. I just knew all of that wasn't for me.

Low and behold I walked in and my mom met me. It sure was a joy to see my mom and my sister. After all the hugs and kisses, they walked me into a full auditorium. There wasn't an empty seat and the biggest applause rang out as I walked in the door. It was a good feeling to be recognized by my family and friends.

People I hadn't seen for years was waiting for me to sign their books. It was so much fun. Some of them had several books for family members and friends who couldn't make it.

They told me how much they enjoyed reading my book and hoped to read the second one if I found the person. I graciously thanked everyone and told them to look out for book number two. It took a while to sign that many books but I wasn't complaining. I had found my calling in life. I wasn't sure until now.

Mom and my sister was so proud. We wrapped things up and made sure I let the principal know how much I appreciated her letting us use the school. She was more than happy to do it and more than proud of me.

I told my mom and sis that I would take them out to dinner because I knew that they were exhausted and did not want them to cook.

Mom said, "Let's go by the house first and freshen up a bit. Then we will go to this new bar-b que place downtown."

When we got home, I got that feeling again that I hadn't had in a long time… like something was going to happen at any time. Mom went in before me. When I walked in the door, more friends that I hadn't seen in years was waiting for me and a spread of all of my favorite foods and more.

Mom got me good. As I walked through the living room, which was not that big, there walked out of our kitchen but the biggest surprise, Ms. Lambkin. We ran into each other's arms at the same time. It was such a joy and surprise to see her face again. "What are you doing here?" I said.

"I wouldn't have missed this for the world. Your mom called and told me about your book signing and here I am."

I could have squeezed her to death. I loved this lady just as much as I loved my mom. I was very fortunate to have her in my life.

I thanked everyone for coming. I signed books, of course, after we stuffed our faces with so much good food. My mom was one cool lady. She knew that I loved the sound of a classical guitar. She had a guitarist to play in the background while I read excerpts from my book. It was a day to remember.

While we were having a good time, we heard a knock at the door. My mom went to the door and, as she was talking, I heard her say, "Hold on. I'll get him for you."

Who could it have been? I had seen just about everyone I knew, except my father. This would be a surprise if he came. He was so busy with his other family but who knows? Maybe he had a change of heart.

This person I was not familiar with but people were reading my book. Maybe she just wanted an autograph. I knew you had to be careful. Everyone who came around did not always have good intentions.

I moved, a little hesitant, as I went to the door to see who asked for me by my given name, Jerome. Everyone who knew me called me Rome. I hardly heard my given name except when Mom was angry with me about something. Then you would hear "Jerome Spencer" and that was it for me.

Part 2

JEROME SPENCER'S LOVE LIFE

CHAPTER

7

MRS. DIXON

I knew that all of the people in the house were people that I had known over the years. This was a stranger and I was kind of leery as to what she wanted. I was a bit nervous but I knew I had no baby mommas anywhere, so it couldn't be too bad.

I signed her book, anxious to hear what she had to say. Then she blurted out, "I believe my daughter is who you are looking for."

This perked my ears up. I had waited a long time to hear someone say those words. Even if it was a witch hunt it was so exciting. Again, that feeling I had in my heart years ago was back. I wanted to hear her story so much.

"Are you the lady that wrote the newspaper?" I asked.

"Yes, it was me but I didn't want to tell the paper anymore. I wanted to talk to you first. So, when I heard you were coming home I knew I could get my chance. I have to start from the beginning in order for you to understand where I am coming from. Do you have the time?"

"Oh, I've got the time. Can I tape this so that I don't miss one word?

"I could be wrong."

"But if you are I will destroy the tape."

"OK."

"Please have a seat while I say good bye to my guests," I said. I told mom what was going on and she knew what to do so I didn't have to worry about my guests. Mom had that under control. She was one of the politest people but when it came to ending a party she did it with so much grace that no one would get offended. I believed that even if she was rude they would overlook it. People liked her.

I retrieved my briefcase from the car and went out to the patio and from then on, I heard one of the most fascinating stories. I left this lady believing that her daughter sounded like a beautiful person. Either way I wanted to meet this lady someday.

The story she told me started off like this:

> *I was married to the most wonderful man. Mr. Dixon is what everybody called him but he was my Doc I called him that because of the way he carried himself tall and was always well-groomed. He looked like a Doctor to me.*
>
> *We met on a blind date. One of my neighbors introduced him to me. It was love at first sight for me. He was older than I was so I wasn't sure if this could become a relationship but it did and, not long after, we got married.*
>
> *Doc worked at a junior high school, grades six through eight which was a nice innocent age. He loved kids. We were hoping to have one or two someday but for now this was good. I was a cook at a college so I had the older kids. We had all the kids we needed to say we were content.*
>
> *But our world changed one day when Doc was working on a Saturday, which he didn't do that often. I believe there was going to be a recognition assembly that Monday, so he was asked if he could work that Saturday, knowing that we could use the money. He had no problem accepting.*
>
> *He went on about his day. He said when he heard the sound of babies cry but it couldn't have been because he was the only one in the building... so he thought. He looked to see if the window was left open and the cry was coming from outside.*

56

He checked that all the windows were locked. By then the cry became louder. It was in the building somewhere. As he followed the sound he found a baby in a basket in the boiler room. How it got there, he had no idea. He was the only person in the building. He started working at seven a.m. and it was about nine a.m. before he heard the cry. The only other people that had keys were the principal and the assistant maintenance worker who was off that day.

He said he was nervous but he picked up the baby to calm it down. It looked like a boy but it was hard to tell. The baby had no hair and was wearing a pretty little white pant suit, so he figured it was a baby boy. He didn't know if he should call the police first or the principal so, of course, he called me and I told him to call the police and that I would call the principal. When the police came, they saw that he was nervous and they took the baby and looked him over.

"It looks like a little boy," my husband said nervously as he watched the police woman take the baby and realized the baby was wet with no diapers in the basket. She looked at Doc. Why? He didn't know but in his heart, he understood: they needed to dry the baby. Doc said the school had some nice white sheets in the nurse office. He went and brought some and told her she could change the baby in his office.

While she took the baby to change it, the other policeman was asking him questions about what time he heard the cry, if he was the only person in the building, and just all kinds of questions that he tried to answer as specific as he could. By the time they were wrapping up the questions, the principal walked in. She knew Doc was nervous and shocked by his ordeal. She hugged him and thanked him for being there.

The police woman came out and asked if the other officer would come into the office for a moment where the baby was being changed. The Principal and Doc looked at each other. They both hoped that nothing was wrong with the child. The officer asked if Doc and the Principal would step into the office. When they did, they saw a smiling baby girl and she had a note that was wrapped in plastic, typed, and put inside her diaper.

They took the proper procedures to see if finger prints were on the baby or anything. It seemed as though who ever placed the baby in the school was very careful no prints were found. The letter was addressed to Doc.

Dear Mr. Dixon,

I am in trouble. I couldn't think of anyone else who could help me but you. You don't know who I am but I have watched you and your wife for years. I love the way that you take care of her and I knew that you would be the right fit to take care of my baby.

Her name is Nadia. She has the biggest black eyes that sparkle. I don't know who the father is because of the lifestyle I was living. If you and your wife would be so kind as to take her and raise her as your own, I would be more than happy and I will feel like I have given her a chance in life that I didn't have.

She is a good baby and I hope she brings you and your wife much joy in your life. From what I see of you, you are a good, caring man and that is the one thing I dream for my child; that, when she grows up, she would find a good man like you. Please let her know some-day that I love her and that you were the best choice to raise her. I give you all legal rights. I cannot give you my real name but I sign off as Jane Doe.

"Wow," the principal said, "Who could this be?"

"I don't have a clue who this could be. I haven't noticed anyone out of the ordinary but how did they get in the building?" Doc said.

"Yes," the principal said. "Who else other than me, Mr. Dixon, and our assistant Maintenance guy, Pedro, who was not scheduled to come in today."

The officer asked for Pedro's number, which they gave to him. They asked him to come down to the police department. They called children services to get the baby until the investigation was done.

The principal asked my husband, because of all of the excitement, if he wanted to go home and she would have Pedro finish the job that day. He said, "No but let me call home and tell my wife what is going on." I was so excited and a little bit scared now. Who was watching us and how did we not see anyone? I peeped out the window just to look at my surroundings but I saw no one out of the ordinary.

I knew Doc would be getting home soon. I ran his bath and had his favorite meal ready. When he came in the door he was smiling from ear to ear as he gave me the biggest hug. I had so many questions for him. He didn't know a lot but one question he did answer was that, if things turned out, we could raise the little girl. Would we be able to? His answer was, "Yes, we will find a way. This is the angel that was sent to us. Wait until you see her. She is beautiful."

After dinner with Doc, I thought to myself that this couldn't be real. I had to call somebody but not get my hopes up too high because the mother could change her mind. I called my sister right away and told her what was going on. I knew she would keep it to herself. She was good like that. Not knowing when the investigation would be over, I started cleaning out one of the rooms to be prepared just in case she would be coming to us. I wanted so much to get her little room ready, so I bought a few things and fixed the spare room that I used for my wash room.

Doc went about his day. Something strange happened that Sunday when my sister came to pick me up for Church. Doc was up and ready to go with us. He usually said he'd go one Sunday but I never pressured him because he was a good Godly man in his ways and that was more important to me.

My sister was amazed with Doc. He was more like a brother to her than a brother-in-law. It was a great service and the ladies could not take their eyes off Doc. I was so proud of him and so proud to be his wife. He took us out to dinner afterward. We had a great day even though I knew Doc had a lot on his mind.

We went about our days: Doc working and me trying to keep the house together and myself from going nuts with worry. Could I really raise a child, especially a girl? I didn't know how to comb my own hair.

It was a fascinating story and I wanted to hear every word of it. I watched her mouth as she talked. It was like I was in a trance. She had all of my attention. Mrs. Dixon continued:

To make this long story short, it took a while before the investigation was over. They didn't have any evidence as to who the child belonged to. After a couple of weeks, we got the phone call that everything was cleared.

The social worker wanted to come over and talk with us about the adoption of the child and to check out everything to make sure we were suitable parents. Doc took the rest of the week off and we prepared for the visit and our new addition.

Everything was satisfactory to the social worker so the day for our bundle of joy to come was that Friday. We had everything ready. When I saw that angel, I fell in love at first sight. I felt something special about this child. I knew her mother had a difficult time making this decision. She wanted the child to have a chance for a better life than she had. I'm glad she saw that in us.

Doc and I had little trouble raising Nadia. She was a sweet baby and a kind young lady. She excelled in everything that she did. I knew that she had favor on her life. She went to college to become a nurse and she was exceptional. One of her biggest problems she had in life as an adult was not to trust men. It's like she had this sixth sense about what the wrong man could do to your life. It was like her mom was speaking to her heart.

One day she said, "Mama, I want to meet a man like my dad someday. Until then I am doing OK. I have my work and, as long as you all don't mind, I'll stay right here and take care of you and Dad if you need me." Nadia is such a giver of her-

self. She made our lives worth living, especially my husband's before he died. Doc was so proud of her. He showered her with things that she needed and some things she wanted because he knew one day he would have to leave her and he wanted her to know that she was loved.

That day came when Doc was working for a contractor for the summer to make ends meet. He fell into a trench and died instantly. We were devastated but knew we had to go on. Doc left us a legacy of love and a great insurance policy that I knew nothing about. He was that type of man.

Nadia met a nice young man later on and things were going well for them. Josh wanted to marry her but Doc not being around to give her away brought sadness to her. I promised her it would be OK, that dad would be with her, and we would give her the finest wedding a girl to have.

But she insisted, "No. I want to go to the court house and save that money for you, Mom." She was good like that. She had a big heart.

She did marry Josh, who was the president of a software company. He was good to her like Doc was to me. We had the insurance money from Doc's death and her husband had a great job, so money was not a big problem to raise a family.

Nadia didn't have to work but she insisted on doing something. Being a nurse did not feel right like she thought it would, so she let that go. Instead, she worked for the Boys and Girls Club as a receptionist. They wanted a family but found out that she could not have kids. That was difficult for her to accept for a while but her husband assured her that everything would be alright. He loved her with or without kids.

I was sad for her because I knew how I felt until she came into my life. This is where I believe that my daughter might be your angel. One day she bought this beautiful black and white rain coat. It looked good on her and she was crazy about it. People would compliment her when she wore it. The girls would ask where she got that coat from. She didn't want anyone to dress like her so she would say she didn't remember.

Anyway, one day she came home without that coat and I asked her where it was. She gave me some crazy story about leaving it at work. I knew that wasn't the truth but it was her business. I just couldn't believe it. So, when one of the neighbors told me about the letter that was in her child's paper from Cinnamon High, I suspected strongly that it sounded like my Nadia.

Nadia changed our lives. I know that she changed other people's lives too. We have had such a wonderful life with her. I just have a strong feeling that it was Nadia. She is always helping someone.

CHAPTER
8

MEETING MRS. NADIA

"Well," I said. "That is quite a story. Did she ever bring the coat back home or tell you anything?"

"No, she didn't. She never said a word so I didn't bring it up again. The other thing that got me to thinking about this is that she never wanted to drive even though she could have a brand-new car. She wanted to catch the bus even though she didn't get paid much at her job. She never asked for much but she never had any money from her paychecks that often. I put all of this together this could be my Nadia."

"Thank you so much for telling me this story. I have never heard anything like this before and who knows? Maybe and maybe not. Can I meet her before I leave for New York?"

"I'll have you come to dinner one day so that she won't suspect anything. She is very private. We have to be careful what you ask her, OK?"

"I promise."

"Just let me know what day is good for you and I will set it up."

We agreed on a day and time. I was looking forward to meeting this lady. Maybe I would remember something about her from that day at the bus stop.

I walked Mrs. Dixon to her car. I looked at my watch and saw that it was late. I thanked the woman for her story and said that it gave me something to think about. As I entered the house, I noticed that all the guests had left except for Ms. Lambkin. I apologized for not spending more time with her but let her know the story that I just heard. I knew it was something she would want to hear. I insisted that she spend the night because of the lateness of the hour and that I would see her in the morning.

She agreed to stay. I was so excited and I could not sleep. I tossed and turned on the sofa while wondering if this was the person. What would I do next and if it wasn't would I continue to search? I had so much on my mind. Eventually I must have fallen asleep because I woke up to the smell of bacon, sausage, coffee, and all kinds of good smells.

"Let him sleep," I heard my mom say.

"I am not asleep. How could I be with those smells coming out of that kitchen?"

I hurried to shower and come downstairs because I had so much to share with them. As I came down I noticed everyone was at the dining room table. We hadn't used that table in years. "So, what's the occasion?" I said.

"Boy, we got royalty here," said my mom.

"Oh yeah? Ms. Lambkin is royalty?"

"No," Ms. Lambkin said. "You are. We are so proud of you."

"Wait until you all hear what Mrs. Dixon told me about her daughter. She was the lady that wrote to the newspaper, a while back and she truly believes that her daughter is the lady that we are looking for." I grabbed my plate and packed it with everything that was cooked.

"I see you didn't miss anything," Mom said.

"Oh no, I'm so hungry. I could eat everything you all cooked."

As I sat at the dining room table I took out the tape recorder and turned it on to let them hear the story that was told to me.

We agreed that this was a great story and she could be the one. "Either way," Mom said. "You can take her life and make your next novel if she allows you to."

"That might be a problem. Her mom said that she was very private. So, she might not confess to anything and I am sure she don't want to open up about her life," I said. "Ms. Lambkin, I have a date to go over for dinner on Friday to meet her. Would you like to come with me, after I check with her mom?"

"I would love to come and be moral support for you."

After breakfast, I took some time to see who was left in town from those school days. I found Chuck and he was doing OK. He told me what everyone else was doing and it seemed like things was going well in the school and English class 501 was still doing well.

The Friday to meet Nadia was approaching and I had the OK from her mother to bring Ms. Lambkin. I dressed nicely because if this was my angel, I wanted her to see that she made an impression on my life that day. When we approached the porch Mrs. Dixon was at the door with her big smile. "Come on in," she said. As we entered I saw the most beautiful lady that I had ever seen since my mother and Mrs. Lambkin.

I smiled the biggest smile, showing every single one of my teeth. Her beauty was astounding.

As we entered a tall, well-groomed gentleman stood to shake my hand and said "hello" to me and Mrs. Lambkin. I knew it had to be Mrs. Nadia's husband. Mrs. Dixon introduced us to them and I said "hello," but I could not keep my eyes off Nadia. She had eyes that glowed and a smile that sent shock waves through your body. I am not exaggerating.

I looked up just in time to notice Josh giving me this look like, "I know but she's mine." You could tell he was so in love with her and I could see that I was falling myself. Mrs. Dixon informed us dinner was ready and to come on into the dining room. She did that right on time because I think Josh was going to tell me a thing or two.

The meal was out of sight, everything you could think of to eat. "Mrs. Dixon, this is an outstanding meal," I said.

"Don't tell me. Nadia cooked most of it."

As I looked her way to say, "kudos to the cook," she blushed and it was like I was in the movies. The sun was coming in the window directly on her bronze skin. I wanted her or someone like her.

We retreated to the living room for dessert when Nadia asked, "So, how does my mother know you and Ms. Lambkin?" At this time, Ms. Lambkin jumped into the conversation for the first time. She knew I would mess up everything at this point. She saw how mesmerized I was. In fact, everybody saw it.

"I was Rome's teacher and he wrote a book about a summer experience that he had meeting a stranger who was very nice to him but he never saw her again," Ms. Lambkin said.

"Is that so?" Josh said. I then glanced up into Nadia's big, beautiful eyes to see if there was a reaction from her, but she only smiled and turned her face toward her husband.

I so much wanted to jump in and ask some questions but I didn't remember what the lady looked like or had on but I do remember her smile and to me this was the smile I saw but I could be wrong so I left it alone.

"I would like to read your book," both she and her husband said at the same time.

"I have a couple of copies in the car. I'll get one for both of you."

I went to the car wondering if this could be the lady. All I remember from that day was her smile. This lady had a beautiful smile, but I wasn't sure if it was her. I gave a book to Ms. Nadia. "You must sign it," she said. So, I did. I wrote, "To Ms. Nadia from a dear friend." I wanted to write, "To the love of my dreams," but I knew better.

When I handed Josh his book he asked, "How much do I owe you for the books?"

"No, this is on me for giving me some of your time and a great meal."

"We appreciate it," Josh said, watching Nadia open the book. "Nadia, what do you think? Is it worth my while to read it?"

"I think so," she said and he laughed.

"You will like it," I said to him with a smile.

We thanked them for their hospitality. As we were headed home Ms. Lambkin said, "You were smitten with that lady, weren't you?"

"You noticed, huh? I could not stop staring. Isn't she beautiful? I tried to keep my eyes off her but I couldn't."

"Yes, she is and so polite. I am sure if she is not who we are looking for, she's done some great things in her life for others."

"I am sure too but I didn't want to pressure her. We will chalk this up as a fun adventure and move on. I am so glad that you came with me, Teach."

"Oh, you moved to New York and now I'm Teach? You don't know my name? By the way, when are you going to introduce us to your girl? I know you have one or two."

"Believe it or not, Ms. Lambkin," I said as I smiled. "I have no one special in my life I've dated a few but no sparks."

"Your work probably keeps you busy. By the way, how is that going for you?"

"I'm glad you asked. The CEO plans to retire and I am in the running with a young lady for the position. Can you believe it?"

"One thing that I have learned about you. When you saw that you could do a thing you put your all into it to make it a success and anything that you touch and want you will succeed at it. That is going to be one lucky young lady when you find her or when she finds you. When you least expect it, she will be the one."

"How do you know all of this?"

"Because it happened to me once in my life."

Now this was the first time she ever talked personal. I wanted to know her story so I asked. "Not now but maybe one day I will tell you," she said. "All I could say now is, when she finds you, hold on to her and be kind."

Ms. Lambkin left for California that morning. I was so glad we had that time to spend together, but I forgot all about Mom. I told her how sorry I was and about the meeting that we had at the lady's house and how we met her daughter Nadia and on and on.

Mom saw that I was so excited and hoped this would be the lead that I was looking for. I spent a few more days with Mom before it was time to get back to work.

It was great being home. It was so much fun at the book signing and meeting people, from grade school to grandmothers, who were reading my book and said they liked it. Thinking about what Ms. Lambkin said, it was time for me to at least consider looking for a special friend. That was all I am looking for right now. If it turned to be more, so be it. I wouldn't fight it.

Ms. Lambkin was the type of lady I wanted. She was kind hearted and so smart. I wondered if anyone did her wrong. Who could hurt a lady like that? I remember something that Tyrone's dad told us once.

He said that in life you will run into girls, women, chicks, and ladies and you will learn the difference. But always choose the lady.

Tyrone's mom was a lady, so why did he do what he did? If he was here I would ask him. I hadn't had that much experience with either, so how would I know? Knowing me, I would probably end up with a chick. Maybe I could help her be a lady.

CHAPTER
9

GIRL OF MY DREAMS

Months had passed and I was looking forward to working hard while climbing up the ladder to success in the office. I heard it through the grapevine that our Editor in Chief was leaving to spend more time with his family. I wanted that job so that was an inspiration to really do my thing and show the CEO that I could handle the job if given a chance.

I wasn't the only person shooting for that job. I found out that one of the other editors who started working there the same time that I did also had her eyes on it. I thought to myself that she probably would get it because she was definitely smarter than I was. She would edit several books in one day and didn't have to redo them. I did run into several problems with my editing when I first started and had to do it over but who knew? We would see.

I worked hard to make a good impression on the CEO. Every paper I edited was on the money. I knew this job would be mine. I felt reassured that I could relax awhile. I decided to go to lunch for a change, something I did not do since I started the job. A cup of coffee and a bagel was lunch most of the time. It was clear to me that in order to succeed you had to work hard and give it all that you have, so I found little time for a lot of things. I ate when I felt hungry and that seemed to work for me. Everyone in the office would go to the deli down the street. I heard that they had good coffee but the food wasn't so great.

I figured it was time for me to check out this deli. I locked my desk and headed out of the door. I could always use a good cup of coffee. The deli was full of all of the people from the office buildings in the area. I wasn't surprised but realized why I didn't go in the first place. I had a lot on my mind as I went into the deli and looked for a table that was empty, not that I was trying to be unsociable. I wanted to eat in peace. I just wanted to eat, read the paper, and get back to the grind. My trip to Ohio was still on my mind when I saw a group leave their table. I grabbed it before anyone else could, being selfish, which was not really my nature. I spread all my work out across the table because I didn't want to be bothered.

"What are you having?" this voice said.

"I'll take a cup of your coffee. What can I eat in this place?" I asked while glancing up to see this big, beautiful eyed doll looking at me. I then looked at the mess on the table and began to move it to my briefcase, not wanting her to think I was a slob.

"What do you have a taste for?" she asked. I wanted to tell her that I heard that the food was not great but, in case she was the cook, I said, "I prefer a steak and potato but I'll take your suggestion."

"We do have a good meatloaf meal. You want to try it?"

She didn't know I would try anything she suggested. As she took my order, I couldn't help but to look at her beautiful hands; nails manicured to perfection. This was the one. My dream girl. She probably had someone. She didn't have a ring on. I made sure I looked at that finger. Nowadays people don't wear their wedding rings, so who knows?

As she was coming with my lunch I said, "That smells great."

"I hope you like it. This is about the best thing on the menu."

"So, what I heard was true."

She laughed as she moved on to her next customer. I quietly said a prayer before I took a small bite of what was before me. It wasn't that bad. I was hungrier than I thought and cleaned the plate. I wanted to take the bread and sop up the gravy but she was on her way back to get the payment. "I see you enjoyed that," she said.

"I did but a big T-bone would have been better," I said, hoping she would say something like, "I could arrange that." The place was busy so she had no time to waste with me. I gave her the ticket and thanked her.

Walking back to my office, a promotion did not seem that important to me anymore. I wanted a wife and family. I wasn't getting any younger. I had a successful job, took care of my mom, and had a novel under my belt that was going pretty good. It wasn't on the best seller list but people were enjoying reading it.

I continued to work hard but I made sure that I went to lunch several times a week just to see this young lady. I didn't always get her when I went in so, to make her notice me, I always gave whoever waited on me a big tip. Women liked to talk, so I knew that would get them talking in the back.

It worked now. Every time I came into the deli they would welcome me at the door. I guess the manager saw what was going on, so one day he came to take my order. He saw the look on my face like, "I don't want you. How do I handle this?" I was polite and ordered only a cup of coffee and a bagel. He came back with my order. I could see the ladies as they waited on the other guests wondering if I was going to give him a big tip.

As I finished my coffee and bagel, I motioned for my ticket. The manager came out and gave me my ticket with a note on it that said, "Thank you for your business. I have never seen my workers work so hard and with a smile. It was because of your kindness. This one is on me." I wanted so much to ask him about one of his workers, but I did not want to seem too anxious and ask too much too soon. Things was smooth sailing and it could not be more beautiful.

Now I had the whole place eating out of my hand, except the one I was trying to impress. She saw right through me and she was not impressed. You see, I didn't give her a big tip the first time I came. She told them in the back that I was cheap.

This proved her wrong. By now, I was pretty cool with the manager and we had great conversations when I came in. I never asked about this lady, figuring that my thought was right. She had someone. She was being nice to me the first time I came in because that is her way.

"By the way," the manager said during one of our conversations. "Why didn't you give Bianca a big tip like you gave the other girls?"

"That's her name? I wanted to see her reaction, first of all, and, man, I want to marry that lady someday. Does she have anyone?"

Now, this had been several weeks that I had come in to the deli and I had never asked about her. "I wondered when you would ask about her," the manager said. "I see the way you look at her. She is a nice young lady. I'm not sure if she has someone or not. She is very private. She does her work and goes on her way."

I wanted to ask more questions but this was enough for now. I had time. I was sure now that I was fine with the position that I was in. If it was meant to be it would be. I was still doing well at the job. If I got the promotion now, that was OK and if I didn't, it was OK. I had something more important on my mind and it was so thrilling. I dated a few females but nothing special. I think they were both looking for someone to have kids with and that was not in my plans at that time. I didn't lead them on. I just let them know that it was the wrong time and I couldn't dedicate myself to anyone yet with my work schedule.

I found out that Bianca was called Ms. B for short, I liked that. The next time I was going in for lunch I would get my nerves up to ask her out. She could only say yes or no. That Wednesday was the day. I made sure I was dressed nice and even went to the dentist, nothing gets a lady like a man with fresh breath and some pearly white teeth. When I walked into the deli the table I usually sat at was free, so I made my way over. As soon as I sat down, Ms. B came over.

She had an attitude. "I heard you give out big tips to the waitresses here. What am I? Chopped liver?"

"No, No. I want to marry you so that you can get all my money."

"You don't even know anything about me. How are you going to marry me?"

"Well, tell me all about yourself over dinner this evening. Then I can marry you."

"You might be a stalker or something. Or have baby mommas all over the city, for what I know."

"Well, let's have dinner and I will tell you all about myself."

I was putting it on strong. My courage was up and I wouldn't take no for an answer unless she told me she was married.

"What do you want? I have other customers," she said.

"Give me some coffee and I'll pick you up here at seven forty-five p.m."

"No," she said. Then I began to beg. By now, we noticed everyone was looking and laughing at us. She smiled the biggest smile and said, "OK."

I got my coffee and headed back to the office. Hunger was no longer on my mind. I could eat later with my wife to be.

She didn't realize I said I would meet her at the deli so that she could build some trust. I didn't ask for her address or her phone number. That's what the other guys do. I would get that later.

Of course, I couldn't wait until time to get off, so I wrapped it up for the day at about three thirty. The young lady in the office who was after the same promotion that I was said, "You leaving early?"

That was something I had never done the entire three years I worked there. It wasn't her business. "There's a first time for everything," I said as I rushed out the door.

10

OUR FIRST DATE

I wanted to be early so I got to the deli around seven fifteen. This was so I had time to get the bubbles out of my stomach and shoot the breeze with the manager before she showed up. To my surprise she was already there, dressed in some nice fitting jeans and a purple blouse. "You're here so early," we simultaneously said to each other as our eyes met.

We both laughed, realizing the other was just as nervous. Since I had made the appointment for the steak house for eight o'clock, this gave us time to hang out at the deli for a while

"I'll be right back," I said as I ran out to the car and back in with a purple rose, not knowing that purple was one of her favorite colors. I could tell she was impressed. "What flower shop sells purple roses? I've never seen one before," she said.

"You'll be surprise at what I can get. I can lasso the moon for you like George Bailey."

"You are a character."

We made it to dinner and had a wonderful time. It was like we had known each other forever. "This was the making of something good and lasting," I thought and hoped.

I didn't want to rush into anything since this was our first date. I really liked her, but I was anxious to know if she would be my girl or if she was involved with someone else. It was time to find out. As I drove her back to the deli I said, "I had a good time."

"So did I."

"We must do this again. By the way, do you have a boyfriend or a significant other?"

As I asked that question I held my breath for the answer. I wanted her to be mine. After a couple of seconds, she said, "No, I don't. I wasn't looking for anyone at this time."

"When you decide to look for someone, would you consider me? Maybe?"

"You seem to be a nice guy, and have your stuff together, but I still don't know anything about you. Except that you have a good job and are waiting for the right girl to share your life with."

I didn't give her much information about myself. I was so interested in her and neither one of us talked about ourselves much. We enjoyed the dinner and great jazz music. I knew she appreciated the music by the way she bobbed her head to the rhythm and kept tempo with her foot. If I did not know anything else about her, I knew that she enjoyed music. "OK, what do you want to know about me?" I asked. The deli was closing but they let us in while they were cleaning and we talked about our lives until we got kicked out. We had so much in common. We were both from Ohio. Could you believe it? And both from Cleveland at that.

How come I never saw her around anywhere? I wanted to ask but it was getting late. I walked her to her car, wanting so much to give her a good night kiss on those big, beautiful lips. Instead, I kissed her hand, the gentleman that I am.

As I watched her drive away I realized we did not exchange phone numbers. I did want to call her to make sure she got home safe. That would worry me the rest of the night unless I knew for sure. I happened to notice the deli lights were still on. As I knocked on the door the manager came to it. "Man, I forgot to get her number, and I know you can't give it to me, but can you call her and give her my number? Please? I just want to know if she made it home safe," I said.

"You are beginning to be a pest," he said as he laughed. "OK. Now let me lock up." Assured that he would do what he said I headed on home. It was later than I thought but I had to call my mom and tell her about this girl and what I'd been up to. I was telling Mom all about her when a restricted phone call registered on my other line. I usually ignored anonymous calls but it could have been Ms. B, so I hastily told Mom I would call her tomorrow. "Hello," I said in this disguised tone, just in case it wasn't her. Silence on the other end. "This is Rome."

"Hi, this is Ms. B. I got your message and, yes, I am home and safe. That was so thoughtful of you. You're doing all the right things to make me say yes. I'll be your girl on a trial basis and if things do not work out there will be no hard feelings. Alright?"

"I'll accept that. What do you have planned for tomorrow evening?"

"Not much. I am off on Fridays, so I am going to shop a little. What are your plans for tomorrow evening?" she asked.

"I plan to be with you."

"OK, here's the deal. Meet me at the Artisan Lounge on Detroit at seven thirty. No questions asked."

She trusted me. Now it was my time to trust her. Just in case, I would call my mom and let her know where I would be and who I'd be with, just in case something funny happened. She was a nice lady and I felt comfortable with her enough to trust her.

I prayed, "Please don't let her have a split personality." I had heard some horror stories from other guys about pretty women who turned out to be nothing but trouble.

I was doubting myself now, not having much experience with a lot of ladies. Would I be good enough for her? She was a classy lady and I liked that so I put those doubts right out of my head. As I got back to the job, I was wrapping up the assignment that I was working on when the CEO popped his head in my office. "I am watching you, young man. Your work is getting better and better. The clients are asking for you lately. Keep up the good work," he said.

What did he say that for? My head was already big like my daddy's. Now it was bigger. But I didn't care. My life was rolling in a direction I never dreamed of. Before I left the office for the day, I called Mom and told her about my date. She told me to be careful and to call her when I got home.

It was five o'clock with plenty of time to get home and chill out for a while. I had never been invited out by a lady before. This was new to me. How should I dress? I had never been to this lounge before. Would we eat? I was clueless, so I grabbed a can of V-8 juice just to satisfy my stomach so it would not have a conversation all by itself.

I pulled up to the club and the parking lot was packed. I went inside the bouncer asked my name. Thinking to myself, *Why did he ask my name?* Then I thought that everyone else must be regulars. *Don't trip, Rome,* I thought, still having a conversation with myself. *Just go with the flow.*

I did as I was told and he sat me at a table in the front of the club. In the table was a dozen white roses and a note from Ms. B. It said: Thank you for a beautiful first date. Sit back and enjoy.

Sit back and enjoy what? I thought. The flowers were beautiful but where was she? Where was Ms. B? Someone from the next table said, "We didn't get any flowers. You must be special." Before he could finish the word special, a waiter came over with a bottle of wine and asked how I liked my steak.

It dawned on me she had everything planned out down to the meal. This chick was exciting. Steak dinner, wine, and roses! I felt like royalty! The only thing that was missing was my date! I placed my order for a steak cooked medium rare. Now all I needed was to see my girl. As my eyes began to pan the room full of dining patrons, I looked for Ms. B and expected to see her walking toward my table through the sea of laughing faces seated at the tables.

The house lights were turned down and the MC said, "Introducing a new act: Ms. B and the Divas." Hold up! Wait a minute! What was going on? Did he say what I think he said? Ms. B and the—who? Ms. B!!! Ms. B!!!! Ms. B stepped onto the stage, looking so good and wearing my favorite colors: gold and white. They started to play some jazz. She was on the saxophone blowing away. It was awesome. After several songs they took a break. She came down to my table and gave me the biggest hug. "Now what do you think of that?" she said.

"You made my day from the dinner to the beautiful music. Why didn't you tell me you played in a group and that you play the sax too?"

"You had your surprises and I have a few up my sleeve."

She was getting compliments from everyone. I could tell the guys wanted her but she was mine. I was going to do everything I could to make that happen.

I thanked her for the roses and told her that it was my job to shower her. She had a free spirit about herself that gave me goosebumps every time I was near her. "So, does this mean you are my girl?" I asked.

"Not yet. We will see."

She went up to play another set for the night. What a night. I was glowing at this point. The dentist did me justice. My pearly whites were shining all over the place. After the show, I walked her to her car. I knew she had to be exhausted.

I didn't push. The wine had me feeling a little sleepy anyway and I needed to get home safely myself. I was able to get a little kiss on the jaw from her this time. "I sure appreciate what you did tonight," I said.

"I thought you would."

This time she called to see if I was home safe. We said our good nights and that we would talk tomorrow.

CHAPTER

11

MEETING HER MOTHER

We talked for a short bit on Saturday. I had to catch up on my house-
work and washing. I could have got a maid but mom taught me how
to take care of a house. Ms. B had some things to take care of herself
which was OK. I didn't want to feel needy and push her away.

This felt good, something to look forward to. I had more time
to talk to Mom now and I was telling her about the date that she
took me on. Mom wanted to know when was I coming home and
bringing the young lady with me. "Mom, I don't know. We haven't
talked about our families yet," I said.

"Does she know that you wrote a book?"

"I haven't had a chance to tell her about that at all but I will."

Sunday was a good day for a picnic. I called her at about nine
p.m. on Saturday just to check on her and see what she had planned
for Sunday. "We are going to Church in this house, so that's where
we will be from eleven a.m. until about two p.m. on Sunday," she
said. We? Did she have a kid? She never said anything about her
home life, so who knows? I should have known that she was spiritual
or something. She didn't show any signs of selfishness.

"You and your kid?" I asked.

"No, my mom. I live with my mom."

"OK. What church and can we hang out afterward?"

"Yes," she said but then asked the question I hoped she wouldn't
ask. "You don't go to Church?"

"It's not that I don't. I just never took the time out to attend
but I do believe. I would not be where I am now without somebody's

help. Can I pick you up around four, if that would give you enough time to get ready?"

"Yeah and then you can meet my mom."

That is usually a good sign when they want you to meet moms. It was like a dream after meeting Ms. Nadia, seeing how stunning she was. I did not think that I would meet another stunning woman, especially one interested in me. With that thought I made a move that would make her mom separate the men from the boys when she met me.

When they got to Church I was already there, sitting in the back waiting for them. Bianca and her mother looked gorgeous; I was not the only one checking them out.

I could tell she was happy to see me. "What are you doing here? You didn't tell me that you were coming," she said. I smiled and looked toward her mom, so she introduced me. We did "hello's" and "glad to meet you.". Following the "preliminaries," we just enjoyed the service together.

After Church, I said, "By the way, ladies, what's for dinner?"

"That was bold," Ms. B said. "Just inviting yourself to dinner. We didn't cook yet."

"I would love to take you both out for dinner, if that's OK with you and your mom. Nothing fancy. So, if you would like to stop by your house and change, I could follow you home and wait outside for you."

"You are welcome to come follow us and relax downstairs while we girls get it together."

That's what I wanted to hear anyway. The house was just as beautiful as they were. My colors all over the living room: gold and white. I'm sure they didn't have much company; everything was immaculate.

"Would you like a glass of water or something?" Ms. B asked.

"No, thank you."

"By the way, you are welcome to look around."

It was like she read my mind. "You all have a lovely home," I said.

"Thank you," her mom said. "Bianca's dad got this home for us and furnished it. All we had to do was move in."

"He has great taste," I said.

After I didn't get a response to that statement I figured that something must have happened. I would just leave that alone. I looked around and, yes, the place was beautiful from the kitchen to the basement.

I didn't dare go upstairs where the ladies were changing. Things were going better than I planned. This was good for now.

As the ladies came down the stairs they both looked so beautiful. "Very impressive home you have here. Your husband really has great taste," I said again, hoping to get more of the details from Bianca this time.

"Yes, he did," Ms. B's mom said. So, that told me he was either dead or they were divorced like so many homes, but I couldn't see any man leaving these two beautiful ladies. Unless there was a side to both of them that I had not seen yet.

"Are you ladies ready?" I asked.

"We're ready but where are you taking us?"

"Trust me. You all will enjoy yourselves."

They looked at each other in sync. "Oh yeah?"

"If this will make you feel better, I will ride with you all. Just follow my directions."

I got in the back seat and gave her mom directions. "Where are you taking us? I have never noticed these streets before and I've lived here a while," she said.

"Trust me. I got you. Now, take this left turn here and park in front of that big white house."

"Is this where you live?"

"Maybe and maybe not," I said as I got out and opened the car door for Ms. B and then rushed to open the door for her mom.

As we went into the big white house they were amazed at all the art on the walls and the décor. I led them to a room that had a table set for three.

As I sat them at the table, a waiter came out with a bottle of champagne. "What's the occasion?" Ms. B asked.

"Just meeting you two beautiful ladies is occasion enough for me." I saw the gleam in Ms. B's mom's eyes and I thought I saw a little tear.

"Look around," I said. "It's OK. That is why I brought you here. I love this place. It is so fascinating."

They were discussing the décor and I explained to them how this building belonged to my boss's family who was born and raised in Spain. "His parents bought the building and had all the furnishings and paintings shipped from there. Only elite people on the guest list are allowed to come in and use it for different functions," I said.

"They must be loaded. This place is beautiful," Ms. B said. "So, are you of that elite status or did he allow you to use the facilities because you are his best employee?"

"A little bit of both," I said. As I laughed they knew better. They weren't paying attention to the group of people setting up a buffet on the other side of the room.

As they were checking out the walls and ceilings, I asked, "Are you ladies ready to eat?"

"Yes," Bianca's mom said. "I don't want to leave this place. I love it."

"You do not have to. Just walk this way." I took them to the back of the house where tables were set up along the walls with a spread of food from all over the world.

"This is amazing, isn't it, B?" I said.

"Yes, it is."

I picked up my plate and commenced to piling up different food. they followed suit. You would have thought I had two teenagers on my hands, saying, "taste this, taste this." For about twenty or so minutes, all you could hear was giggles and, "this is good" as though I was not in the room. I never laughed so much.

I had them just where I wanted them now. I wanted them both to see and know that I was a gentleman and I only had good intentions for them. It was like I was on a mission to show these ladies that good things do happen.

CHAPTER
12

BIANCA'S STORY

When they finally settled they, of course, had questions as to how I arranged all of this. I let them know that I had a good relationship with my boss and he allowed me to use the place for that day when I told him how special they were to me. "The food was prepared by chefs. I told them what I wanted and they did a great job of preparing everything," I said, "By the way, you both seem to know the names of those paintings on the wall."

Abruptly, Bianca's mother began to sob hysterically. She could not compose herself. Bianca put her arms around her mother to console her hesitantly, and Bianca told me the story of her father, who was from Barcelona, Spain.

> *While he was living in Cleveland, Ohio, he met my mom. They began to date and soon my mom learned that she was pregnant. She found out that he had a wife and family.*
>
> *My mom was so hurt and she also was so in love with him. His wife knew about my mom but my mom did not know about her or that he had a family at the time. He always came to our little apartment on West 25th street. Mom never questioned him. When we needed something, he was always there.*
>
> *When she asked him about it he said that, yes, he had a family but he also loved her and me and*

did not want to leave us. My mom accepted that and he kept doing what he was doing, and still taking care of us.

One day my mom got an anonymous letter in the mail saying that she was dealing with the wrong man. That someone would try to hurt her if she did not let him go. My mom showed Carlos the letter. He had an idea as to who wrote it. He told my mom that he would have to lay low for a while. He wasn't sure if this person was serious or not. So, I knew our lives would never be the same again.

I was devastated when they told me; I was hurt that I would not be able to see my dad for he took me to my classes every afternoon when he got off from work. I never knew what kind of work my father did and I still don't know to this day.

We had to move back to the eastside of Cleveland where my mom could get a part-time job at the Boys and Girls Club on 139th street tutoring. I couldn't go to the school anymore for violin lessons.

It was like my whole world was over. Having a hard time accepting our lifestyle, I started to act up a bit in school. Mom thought it would be better that I come to her job straight from school to do my homework, whether I liked the idea or not. She was so disappointed in my behavior and she knew she had to get a handle on it.

I did as she said. While doing my homework, I started talking to the receptionist at the desk every day. She was so nice.

I found myself opening up to her about my life and she listened. I know she probably got sick of me whining about how we had to move, how I couldn't continue my violin lessons, and so on but she never complained or pushed me away.

I now liked coming to work with Mom. I had someone to talk to and I was getting my homework done at the same time. One day that I was talking to her, I told her how I wanted to learn to play the guitar but we couldn't afford to get one.

She told me how she had a guitar that she didn't need and she would bring it to me the next day. I was so excited! I finished my homework just in time for Mom to come. I told her about the lady bringing me a guitar. She saw my excitement but was quick to point out two things: I had to get my attitude together and how would I pay for lessons?

I wasn't worried. I would teach myself the guitar. I promised her I would get it together.

On the way home, I was so pumped about this guitar. Of course, my mind wondered, "What if it's not in decent shape? I can't afford to get it repaired. What if she forgets or changes her mind? Some people say stuff at the time and change their mind when you are out of their sight."

I had enough disappointments for now. Then my mind said, "She doesn't seem like that type of lady that would lie to you," even though I didn't know anything about her. All I talked about was myself and my problems. When we got home we had dinner and we both were exhausted and went to bed early.

The next day in school I was no trouble. My teacher was kind of concerned and asked if everything was OK at home or if I wasn't feeling well. I informed her that I was fine. I tried not to get so excited when it was time to go to Mom's job just in case the lady did not come through.

As I walked into the building she had that big smile on her face and handed me a beautiful guitar case. When I opened it, I saw the most beautiful guitar I had ever seen. It was acoustic, just what I wanted.

"Are you sure? This is beautiful," I said.

"Yes," she said. "Here is some sheet music that goes with it."

I hugged her so tight and thanked her tremendously. People were always at her desk for help with something. I saw that she was busy, so I got out of the way but I saw the tears in her eyes as she wiped them away. She was happy that I was happy. I did my homework as usual while guarding that guitar with my life.

Mom glanced out of her class for a moment. With a big smile on my face, I held up the guitar. She smiled back. She knew I was content, at least for now. She already felt bad for what had happened to us. This was a good thing.

Not too long after that day Mom got a phone call from my dad telling her to pack up all of our clothes. He didn't care what she did with the rest of the things because he had a plane ticket for both of us to move to New York.

She tried asking him questions about where we would live and etc. but he only said, "Trust me. I have everything covered. Get a taxi and give them this address."

It was bittersweet. I wanted to be with my dad but I had grown fond of the Boys and Girls Club, especially that lady. And I was doing good in school now. Things were looking up for us.

Before we left I finally asked my mom what the receptionist's name was that gave me the guitar. Even though I talked to her every day, I never knew her name. She said, "Call her Ms. Nadia."

Mom didn't know her last name or if she was married or not. Anyway, I wrote a thank you note to *her and told her how I would miss her and I would take very good care of the guitar, which I did.*

Mom sold everything except what we would take with us and there we were in New York with a paid for home that my dad furnished and everything like he said.

We were just as glad to see him as he was to see us. Mom had so many questions for him about what happened. After we saw the beautiful place that he had for us, my mom and I relaxed while my dad was in the kitchen. He said, "Sit down and rest. I have dinner for you."

He was a good cook. I think that's one of the reasons my mom wanted to be with him. He was a smart man. He gave my mom a checkbook with enough money to hold us up for a while until she found a job, which he knew she wouldn't have a problem with.

"I can't stay with you," he said. "I will be back as often as I can."

We cried and hugged him. We didn't want him to go but had to accept it. That we did. So, I got a job at the deli and mom is working at Saks Fifth Avenue, which is right up her ally. She loves fashion, as you can see.

"Wow, that was so noble of your father to make sure you all had a place to stay," I said.

"Yes, it was, but we might not see him again. I am sure his wife is keeping a tight rope on him. He does write from time to time but we cannot write back. He said not yet."

By this time, they both were in tears, so I changed the subject to focus on what I had planned for us next before we called it a day. It was a balloon ride and we had so much fun. I wanted them to forget about their troubles. They didn't have Carlos but they had me now and I would take care of them. I also wanted to use this time to bring up the book I wrote and the lady named Ms. Nadia that I had met who also worked at the Boys and Girls Club. Was this the same person?

Since we were having so much fun I decided to wait until another day. We finished the day off and they both thanked me with many, many hugs and kisses. I liked that.

I looked forward to a date with just me and Ms. B. The next couple of days we would try to fit one in. It was time for the boss to pick a predecessor. Both Lisa Gillman and I had competed for the position for several years now. Lisa Gillman had always been my main rival. The only person that could upset my placement on that pedestal was Lisa Gillman. I had accepted the fact that it might not be me and it was OK. I had a life now. I was fine where I was now and my first book was doing well.

The CEO was ready to make his decision as to who he would choose for his predecessor. He called both of us to his office. At this point, I was fine with not getting the position, if that was the case. My life had changed a bit. Work was not the only thing I had in my life. He said I had become a great editor and he knew that, if put in his seat, I could do the job, but it would be beneficial for him and the company to go with the other party. Looking at her background in Business, she had the knowledge for the job. I understood his position and why he had to choose her. It was OK. I was not upset but then he through a curve at me and said how much the company depended on me.

He wanted to promote me to head editor which meant that everyone had to bring their work to me to approve before it went to the big office. That was an honor and not bad pay either. It was still a pressure position but it freed me up to have a life. I was so excited and thanked him for believing in me.

What a morning! I could not wait until lunch time now to see Ms. B and tell her the good news. I was falling for this girl so fast and I wasn't sure if she felt the same way. It was so early in the relationship but I still knew that she was the one I wanted to settle down with. I just hoped she felt the same way I did.

I had no time to waste. I was getting older and I had so many dreams and goals, but I wanted to share it with someone. Hopefully I had found that someone.

I went to the deli to see Ms. B. The place was busy and the atmosphere was very pleasant but something felt out of sorts. The person I came to see was not waiting tables; I asked the manager if I could see Ms. B for a minute but he said, "She had to leave to go to Ohio. Her and her mom. I believe she tried to call you." "Do you know why she had to go to Ohio?"

"No, but she didn't act like anything was wrong. She left this for you," the manager said. He handed me a white rose and a letter. This was amazing. "I loved this girl for sure," I thought as I sat at my favorite booth. One of the ladies brought me my usual. I had friends and it was a great feeling knowing that people liked you. I was anxious to see what Ms. B had to say. I hoped it was not bad news about her father.

It turned out that her father bought her a new car and wanted her to come to get it. So, she and her mother took the bus so that they could drive the car back. She said she would call me later that night and that she was so proud of me. She heard about my promotion. Sounded like she was really my girl and wanted the same thing that I wanted: a lasting relationship.

As I enjoyed my bagel and coffee, thoughts came in my head. She never talked much about other guys in her life. I wondered why. She was a great catch. It didn't matter now anyway. She was mine now and I was going to do my best to keep it that way.

I called Mom as soon as I got home to tell her the good news. She was excited and a little sad. She was hoping I would be coming home someday to stay. She really missed me even though my sister was there. It wasn't the same. She would always say she wanted us both home so she could hug us whenever she wanted to.

I assured her that, with this promotion, I would have more time to come home and maybe do some more book signings. She liked that but she knew she could come here and I would get us a house. She would not hear of it. Her friends were there. That was home.

I understood now because I had found some friends here that meant a lot to me. I asked to buy her a new house. She always said, "For what? This house is enough for me." I just wanted to do something to show her how much I loved and appreciated her.

CHAPTER
13

A TWIST OF FATE

Ms. B called around ten p.m. that night. I was getting a bit nervous," I said.

"I am sorry. I was so busy with my father. He didn't have a car waiting for me. He took me to pick out what car I wanted and then he took me and my mom out to dinner."

"You all had no trouble with his wife?"

"No. She was out of town visiting her family, so we have the whole weekend together."

"I miss you," I said before I knew it. I didn't want to seem like I had nothing else to do while she was gone but, in case someone else was checking her out, I needed her to know.

"I miss you too," she said. That was music to my ears. I asked her if she would do me a favor while she was in town. I asked her to go by and see my mother and give her a hug from me that way she could meet her finally. She said it was no problem and that she would love to.

I gave her my address and told her to tell her mom hello. I wished I could be in Ohio with them but this was not a good time for me to leave. I had to be at work Monday and they would be gone until Tuesday night. They wanted to visit some of their friends while they were in town. I knew I had better call my mom, even though it was late, just to let her know to expect some company in the next couple of days. My girl was coming by to meet her since she was in Ohio.

I knew she wouldn't mind. This was new to me. I never had a girl that meant enough to me to have her meet my mom, so she knew that this girl had to be OK. I spent my Saturday resting a while then doing some cleaning that was so desperately needed. The apartment was looking good now and I even mustered up energy to get to the gym. I was glad I did. I was beginning to look like a sloppy, young man, after seeing that I was not as buff as some of the guys in the gym. It didn't matter in the past to me about how I looked. I had no one in my life who was important enough to do something about it. Now I did. I had to get this together for the day that Ms. B. would say I do.

It was a good workout. I was feeling like a king. At this time, my life was good. Things was going well. I dared not to wonder if this would change for the worst. You know when things are going so well that you can talk yourself into the opposite? I kept my spirit up knowing that my girl would meet my mom and I knew mom would fall in love with her like I did.

I waited for the phone to ring later that night, looking to hear from Mom or Ms. B. I heard from no one. I wanted so much to pick up the phone and see what was happening but my gut said that they were having a good time. They would call me tomorrow. Following my gut, I turned in early, looking forward to all of the exciting things my mom would have to say. At least I hoped it was exciting. I only knew how exciting she was with me. Even though we had not spent a lot a time together, she and her mother looked like they had class. I knew when I went into their home, and saw the way Ms. B's father had laid it out, that they were accustomed to the finer things in life. Sunday was never one of my favorite days. We didn't grow up going to Church because Mom worked on Sundays and we did chores around the house, along with our homework. Now that I was older I felt lost. Then I remembered how I had a nice time at Ms. B's church. Maybe I would go back some Sunday but not that day. I needed to hear what was happening.

The phone rang just as I was about to get in the shower. "Hello?" I said.

"Hi," that sexy voice on the other end said, so I knew it was not my mother.

"Hey, babe. I thought you were never going to call me. How you doing? Are you having a good time?"

"Oh my, yes, sorry. I couldn't call you yesterday. We were so busy. Your mom took us out to what she says was her favorite restaurant and it was so good."

"Momma Blue? Yeah that is one of her favorite restaurants. So, you guys must have hit it off."

Bianca's voice increased in pitch, speed, and volume when she said, "But wait until you hear this! I can't tell you all of it on the phone but your mom gave me a copy of your book. Why didn't you tell me you wrote a book?"

Before I could answer she interrupted. "You will never believe this! The lady that you thought was the person? I know her! That is Ms. Nadia from the Boys and Girls Club that I told you about. Your mom told me and my mom what happened and how Ms. Nadia's mom came over. And you and your teacher went to meet her but she denied being that person. Well, we went over to visit her. She was so glad to see us. She was more than ecstatic when she found out that I was your girl. We had a long conversation and she told me that she was the lady that you had the encounter with at the bus stop but she didn't want any publicity. It was something that she did and thought nothing of it."

"You're kidding me! This is the best news! I knew it was her. I remember the lady had a big smile. Just like Ms. Nadia. Did she say anything else?"

"Well, her husband interrupted her. I noticed he is very protective of her. She said that she owes you an apology for not saying something sooner but she wanted no publicity."

"Did you have a chance to read the book?" I asked.

"I started it. You can write. I'm looking forward to finishing it. By the way, I love your mother. She is so cool. I met your sister too. She is nice. My mom and your mom are already planning our wedding. Can you believe it?"

"I can. I know my mother. I miss you."

"I miss you too. I'll be back Tuesday."

I remembered that my mother's birthday was coming up and that I am always late with sending her a gift. I thought I could get a head start on a project for her. "I was wondering, while you're in town, could you do me a favor? My mom does not want to move but I always wanted to do something special for her. She always complained about her kitchen looking tacky..."

Bianca graciously accepted the challenge. "Don't worry. I know people. I will have my mom take her out for the day on Monday and get this thing rolling."

"Do you have enough money to do this?"

"Yes, I can do this."

"I will owe you forever but I will pay you when you come back."

"Any idea of what she wants?" Bianca questioned.

"I know she wanted to change the cabinets from that tacky old white to something neutral."

"OK, I'll talk to my mom and we will make you proud."

We said our good nights and, boy, a feeling came over me that I could not explain to anyone. To even think that Ms. Nadia was my angel was the icing on the cake for me. I felt that the book readers would want to know but how could I do this? She wanted to be private.

I called my mom who was more than happy to hear from me and wanting me to know how much they, as in her friends along with the family, was crazy about Bianca and her mom. I told her that I knew she would fall for her. She was a special lady.

We talked about the fact that Ms. Nadia admitted to being the lady years ago at the bus stop and how I wished I could at least let the readers know that we found her, but it would be difficult because Ms. Nadia did not want publicity. I asked how she thought I could approach her about it.

My mom suggested I speak with her mother and see what she thought. I thanked her and told her that I loved her and I would be home soon.

Trying not to let the secret out to my mom, we talked about the book and what she was cooking. "Are you cooking some of that good old shrimp and grits for my girl and her mom?"

She said, "I was so embarrassed by this raggedy kitchen, so we went out. I wish I had an advanced notice that they were coming. It would have been a great time to get something done."

"Mom, they are not that kind of people. They are down to earth. It wouldn't have mattered to them. Anyway, this won't be the last time that you will see them. When I come home we will work on the kitchen, OK?"

After telling my mom how much I loved her, I told her I was glad that she and Bianca and her mom were having a good time together. I used that Sunday to do something I hadn't done in a long time; I turned to the Church Channel and listened to preacher after preacher, who blew my mind.

With the teachings that they gave after I had enough in my limited knowledge of the word, I made a nice salad for dinner with some baked salmon and then turned in for the night. I knew that Monday would be hectic. I would start my new position and who knew what problems I would have. The employees who had to report to me might not take it that well. This was something new and people have a hard time with change.

Things went better than I expected. Only one employee gave me a difficult time. He felt that he should have got my position because he had more experience. I called him in the office and informed him that I worked hard to get where I was. So, if he was serious about his future and really liked working at the New York Rising Stars Publishing Company, he should work hard also and learn everything that he could. Who knows where he could be someday? He thanked me after he closed the door. I had always wanted to motivate others like Ms. Lambkin motivated me and many others. I guess all of that motivation on Sunday got way down in me and spoke into my future.

I looked forward to lunch, seeing the gang at the deli, and telling them what Ms. B was up to in Ohio. The place was packed, as usual, and my favorite seat was taken. It was OK. I didn't own the seat. I looked around for another booth when the manager saw me. He went over to the people at my booth and whispered something. They got up, smiling, and he motioned for me to have a seat.

"You didn't have to do that. I could have found another seat," I said.

"That is not the way we treat a famous author. Man, Ms. B told us about your book and we all got a copy. You can write. It is a great story. Now we all want to know if you found the person."

"It's funny you should ask; we might have but we're not sure if she wants to be in the public eye. So, I can't say for now. We will see."

"Can you sign my book before you go? I hate to do that to you on your lunch break."

"Oh, no problem."

"Today I have that meatloaf meal that you liked. Is that OK?"

"Yeah." I was a bit hungry. Eating salad does nothing for a growing man. We need meat. As I waited for my meal the waitresses came out one by one to get their books signed.

Other guests in the deli wanted to know what I wrote. They showed them the book, so now I guessed I would get a new fan base. How cool. Lunch was good. I went on back to work, waiting to hear from Ms. B about how things were going. It was time to call it a day when the phone rang. "Hi, babe, how it is going?" I said, knowing that there was only so much she could do in that little time but whatever she could do I knew it would be great.

"Things are going great. Your mom is out with my mother. Your sister told all of your mom's friends what we were doing and they pitched in. We will be through in an hour and I will send you a video on your phone so that you can see."

"OK, I look forward to seeing it. By the way, have you talked to Ms. Nadia again or her mother?"

"Yes, they are over here also helping. Her husband painted this morning."

"Awesome," I said. "Got to go. I will talk with you later."

It sounded like everyone was on board and it was going to be a success. I knew this girl was the one. When you can trust someone to do something so important for you and they can see your vision… what a catch. I know once Mom saw it that she would be so happy. I went about my day wanting so much to call my mom but I didn't want to say anything to give the secret away.

The time had come finally. Ms. B was on the phone, breathing heavily like a person running for their life. "Ok, I just sent you the video. Call me back and tell me what you think."

The kitchen was amazing! How could they have done that in such a short time? The whole town had to be involved in this. The colors were amazing. The cabinets were brown and the walls were beige. They put in a brand-new table and chairs. It was beautiful. Then the video took me to her bedroom. They managed to paint it and have it match the colors in the kitchen.

This was above what I expected. Everyone was on the video saying hello. At the end they all looked exhausted but like they had a good time.

"Baby, you went beyond my expectations. I love you," I said. Oops. Silence. Then she said, "I love you too."

This was it. We were going ring shopping when she got back. "I have to go now. Your mom will be home in about fifteen minutes and I know she will call you. We will make sure that she knows that this is from you, so call in about a half an hour to give her a chance. And guess what? Momma Blue donated food, so we are going to throw down.

I wished I was there where all the fun was. This was the most excitement that my mom had in a long time. It was well overdue and I know she would be surprised and impressed. Well, it was eight p.m. and I hoped that was enough time. I called and my sister answered. "Hi Rome," she said. "Mom is so happy. She loves it. She cried. Here she is."

"Hi Rome, you made momma so happy," my mom said. "This is beautiful. Everything and everybody was so nice to pitch in. I hope you come home soon. You have to see it."

Mom knew nothing much about technology, so she would not understand that I saw. So, I just said, "I look forward to seeing everything."

She put Ms. B on the phone. "Rome, she loves it. This was a good idea. We are having a great time. My father even pitched in and bought your mom one of those glass tables that we have at our house. Isn't that great?"

It felt like a family get together and the only person missing was me. I wanted to take off that night and be with them but I knew that was not a reality. Ms. B would be home the next day. We would get a chance to go together next time.

CHAPTER
14

THE BIG QUESTION

Tuesday could not come fast enough for me. I had a lot to do at the job, so I put my mind on the projects that were coming in. There was some good projects. I had to send a few back to re-write but it seemed OK. They gave me no trouble. Maybe they heard the conversation that I could be moving on some day and were getting prepared to take my place. Walls do talk, you know.

Lunch time came right on time. I remembered then that I had no dinner on Monday. That meatloaf meal from the deli filled me up and I was not hungry. That never happened before. I told the manager and his staff what happened in Ohio and they were so happy that everything turned out OK. I asked when Ms. B would be back on duty. He said she was working tomorrow. "We wanted to make sure she had some rest since you worked her so hard," he said.

"True that," I said, "And I appreciate it. Now what can I do for you since you're thinking of my future wife's health?"

"I was thinking that this place can use a little more business," the manager said. "When you announce that you've found the mysterious lady, will you do it from here and do a book signing?"

"I would love to. If I can get Ms. Nadia to say it would be OK, I would love to."

"It's a deal. I knew there was something about you when you walked into this deli that day. Things have been better."

"I'm glad to do what I do. See you tomorrow."

I knew Ms. B would be in around six p.m. so I waited until about eight to call to give them a chance to unwind.

"Hey, can I come by for a little while? I won't stay long. It would be good to see you and thank you in person for what you did for my mother," I said.

"Sure. Come on over. I would love to see you too. I have something to tell you anyway."

You know when a girl tells you that it is usually means a baby is on the way but, in this case, there was no way. We hadn't gone there. I looked forward to hearing whatever it was.

I arrived and the door swung open. She ran out to the car in her bare feet and gave me the biggest hug and kiss on the lips. "I missed you so much," she said. "You look good. What did you do?"

"Thank you," I said. "I hung out at the gym a bit." I couldn't tell her I wasn't eating much because of my love for her. That would be too much to put on her. Her mom gave me a hug and said that she was glad to see me and how she loved my family, especially Mom. "Now I see where you get your charm from. Everyone in that city loves your mom," She said.

"That's what I wanted to tell you. Everyone volunteered and donated the supplies that we needed, so you don't have to pay out of pocket for anything," Ms. B said.

"You're kidding me."

"No. Didn't they, Mom?"

"Yes," she said. "Not one of them would take a penny from us."

"Wow, I had no idea mom had that kind of love in the city."

"Speaking of love…" Bianca said as she looked at her mom as if to say, "give us some privacy."

"I'm going to bed. I'll see you guys tomorrow," her mom said.

"How can we love each other so soon? Do you think that this is real?" Bianca asked. She was asking so many questions so fast. It didn't seem like she took a breath. I gave her time to get all the questions that she had out and then I said, "I know a gem when I see one and I don't want to lose you. I allowed you to do something without knowing if you could, for the most important person in my life, and you aced it. I know I want to be with you forever and I know that I love you. If this is going too fast, I'll back off but I won't stop loving you and when you are ready—"

Before I could say, "I want you to be my wife," she interrupted me. "Come and see my car my dad bought!" she said. It was OK. She was afraid or maybe she didn't want to marry. We both was a bit young but I knew what I wanted and hoped she wanted too.

"This is beautiful," I said. Of course, it was a red 2016 Malibu with everything in it. I knew one thing: her father was one man that loved her and I wanted to be the next.

It was getting late, so I let the marriage question disappear for now. "Can we have a date on Friday, if you have no plans?" she asked.

"Sure. I would love to see you."

"OK, we will talk tomorrow. Have a good night."

"You too."

It was not all lost. She asked me out on a date. All was not lost.

We talked the next couple of days, since she had been in Ohio. A buzz was in the air from the family that I was going to ask Ms. B to marry me. Mom knew me well. I don't fool around when I want something. I go after it with all I got.

So, Mom told Ms. Nadia's mom what she thought. This was good news to Ms. Nadia. She had always liked Bianca from a girl when she was at the Boys and Girls Club and thought that I was a good young man like her husband.

She even told her mom how bizarre it was that this happened. "No," her mom said. "This was meant to be, just like you coming into our life. Everything happens for a reason."

Then the next thing mom told me was mind blowing. She agreed to have me announce that I found the angel as long as her husband agreed with her and we did not use her last name.

This was what I needed. I couldn't wait to tell Ms. B what was happening and it was all because of her. We went to her club where she played and had dinner. We talked about so much. She was happy for me that things were going well and that Ms. Nadia agreed to come out if it was OK with Mr. Josh.

Then she told me why she got nervous when I wanted to talk about the M word and all of the reasons why not. She didn't have a great job to contribute and she wanted to pursue her music career. Then she wanted to teach music, which was not a problem for me. I was doing OK financially and writing seemed to be my thing. There were many books in me that had to come out. We could make this work.

"Give me some time," she said. "I was not expecting this at this time in my life."

"Neither was I but it's here and it's real. Why waste life when you know what you want? We can work this out. Unless you have someone else in mind…"

"It's nothing like that. It's you I am concerned about. I understand you have not dated that much. What if after we marry I'm not all that you thought? I don't want to go through the pain that my mom is going through if things do not work out."

I understood where she was coming from. I watched my mom deal with life after my dad left. Even though I knew in my heart that I would be faithful and would not hurt her for all the days of my life, she didn't know me that well. But I hoped she would give us a chance.

I agreed that we would put off the M word until she felt sure I was the one but we would not stop dating as long as she understood that I was OK.

I let her know that I loved her and I knew that we were young. We did not have to get married right away but I wanted her in my life. I also did not want to put pressure on her. "Take all of the time you need," I said. I was not going anywhere.

I wanted her opinion on the idea I had about approaching Ms. Nadia about revealing who she was in a way that she would be comfortable with. I wanted to speak with her husband first to see how he thought it should be done, knowing how protective he was of her. "Why not after spending that little time with them? I know he is protective of her but he is also proud of her too," she said.

"Yes, you noticed that too. The way he looks at her is so nice; to see people can still be in love after so many—" I quickly changed the subject. We were not traveling down that road again.

Now how would I talk to him about it? Would I call him or write a letter? He intimidated me the first time that we met, so I was in a dilemma. I was too afraid to talk with him but I also wanted to get this out to my readers because many inquired if I had found the person, plus I thought that this would be a good time. With the holidays coming, this would fit right in with some of the stories that were on the internet, and in the news. How strangers were helping unexpected people randomly and changing their lives.

This lady seemed to live her life changing lives and it was time that the world knew. Why not? Well, we would see if her husband felt the same way. As I walked Ms. B to her car I said, "I need to go to Ohio to do this in person. Do you think in a couple of weeks that you will be able to take a day off? We can go on a Friday and be back for work on Monday, if that's OK with you?"

"I'm sure I can since the manager just loves you and the girls will do anything for you, the man with the big tips. You can also see your mom's house in person. Is she still happy about it?"

"Happy is not the word. She said she had a brunch and invited the ladies in the neighborhood. She is enjoying that house again."

"Great! Let me know which weekend you would like to go and I'll put in for it."

"Cool. Have a good night. I'll talk to you soon."

I had to call my mom and see if what I was planning was a good idea or not. Of course, she said yes. It had been a while since I had been home and I wanted to see her as much as she wanted to see me.

No more surprises for a while. I didn't want her to have a heart attack or anything with too much excitement.

She was up in age but she told everyone she wouldn't die until she got a grandbaby. My sister always looked at me because she said she was not bringing no babies into this world. It was too rough out here, so that put the pressure on me. The one who had no steady girl or anything but work on his mind at that time.

It was no problem with my boss to get a couple of days off. It seemed that I was working so much and had not realized how many days I had accumulated for vacation. She wondered if I would ever take a break.

Ms. B was able to take off and we were on our way. I was nervous as to how I would approach Mr. Josh, this tall intimidating man. I was sure that he wouldn't want Ms. Nadia to put herself out there to get hurt. No matter how nice we are, we all will have haters. You could tell that anyone that tried to harm Ms. Nadia would be in big trouble with her husband. We made it to Mom's in time for dinner. Of course, she had a spread just the family. This time she didn't tell anyone I was coming. She wanted us all to herself. The place looked great. From the video I couldn't see all of the special touches that Ms. B and the gang had done.

"Mom, this is beautiful," I said. "I hope you love it. I wanted to do something special for one of the woman that I love."

She caught on to that. She had never heard me use the L word with anyone except my sister and her. She knew I was serious about Ms. B and she understood why she was a great catch for me. I was looking for my soulmate. I did not want just a fling. The family sat around the table eating, talking, and laughing while telling her about how goofy I was when I was a boy. What few pictures we had they brought out and, yes, I was goofy but good looking.

Mom knew why I was home, so she told me not to be afraid. "So, if her husband felt her safety would be jeopardized and thought it was not a good idea, respect their wishes and move on," she said. "You might not ever be able to share that with your readers but at least we know, and that is a good thing.

Mom was right as always. The older I got the wisdom that she had really tripped me out. Where did she get it from? After dinner, I called Ms. Nadia's mom and she was glad to hear from me when I told her that we were in town to see Mom and to see if Mr. Josh will allow us to use her name to let the public know about the secret angel.

She said that Nadia was out but Josh was home. "Come on by and talk to him and let's see what he thinks about this idea," she said. I told her that I had Bianca with me and asked if that was OK.

"Of course," she said. "She's like family to us. I am sure that she told you that she knew Nadia when she was a girl. How bizarre that this turned out this way." I let her know that we would be over in about a half hour.

When we arrived, Josh met us at the door. "Come on in have a seat. So, I see you got a nice lady with you," he said. He seemed relaxed and in a good mood. Bianca made a good impression on him.

Maybe she talked about me? Who knows? Whatever. I wasn't nervous anymore.

"My wife told me the whole story about that day. All these years and she never told me anything about the things that you wrote in the book. I knew she had a good heart. That's how I fell in love with her. She was helping someone the time that I met her and I noticed it. Then that smile sealed it for me. I am just concerned about the hateful people in the world and the things they would say. That what she did was nothing and it would hurt her, taking away that sweet spirit that she has."

"I feel the same way, so I will be very careful about how I put her name out there. I will only use her first name and not any of her contact information. I promise you I will never do anything to hurt Ms. Nadia. I feel like I am family too."

"So, how would you do this?" Josh asked.

I was thinking about contacting J. J. Billings on Channel 78 to inform him of what I am trying to do, maybe he will help me out.

Every city had its favorite anchor man and Cleveland was no different. We had J. J. Billings on channel 78. I thought that he would be the best way to go. We would check with Ms. Nadia to see what her thoughts were. "That approach sounds like it would work to me. We will see what my wife has to say about it," Josh said and then shook my hand. I understood his love for this woman in that handshake. It said, "I know you get where I am coming from."

He asked if we were hungry and, of course, I said I was. "Well, let's have dinner. Momma cooked some good chicken and dressing and the works. Nadia will be home any minute. Did you know she still insists on taking the bus even though she has her driver's license and a car? I don't stop her but I do insist that I take her some places just because I want to see what she is up too. But she won't let me."

"Have a glass of sherry?" Nadia's mom asked. At first, Bianca and I said no at the same time and she said, "Oh, it won't hurt you. It will only give you an appetite. You'll be fine. A glass of sherry keeps you young. Look at me in my late seventies and looking fifty."

We laughed as she did a dance to the kitchen. A voice from outside said, "What's so funny?" It was Ms. Nadia.

CHAPTER
15

BIANCA SAYS YES

She gave her husband the biggest hug and started telling him about her day. She was helping a young lady who had limited cooking skills cook soul food. "What did you all cook?" I asked.

"Collard greens and oxtails. That was her husband's favorite. She wanted to surprise him."

"Come on, guys, the food is ready."

"I'll be right in. Let me freshen up a bit." As Ms. Nadia went into the bedroom her husband followed.

Now that's what I was talking about. I wanted that. I knew no funny business was going on but he missed her and probably wanted to give her a bigger kiss in private. I looked at Ms. B and she did the thing that she does best; she surprised me and gave me a big kiss on the lips and then said, "I do." I thought I would die. I knew what that "I do" meant and I could not hold it together.

When we sat around the table, I wanted to blurt it out but I knew we had to get the ring and tell the moms first and, oh, her dad. We had to get his approval first, so this trip worked out perfectly. I kept my cool. The dinner was out of sight. This lady could throw down. I ran the idea by Ms. Nadia about how I would go about revealing her to my readers. She approved. I thanked her and her husband, now my buddy, and gave her mom a big kiss on the cheek for that great meal.

Now it was time for one other thing I had to do before I left Ohio; it was time to meet Ms. B's father and ask for her hand in marriage. "Do you think we will be able to see your father today?" I asked.

"He's probably at work, knowing him. I'll give him a call," she said. She asked if he would have anytime to meet her after he got off, which he said yes and asked why she didn't tell him she was in town. She told him that she would tell him all about it when she saw him.

"Can we meet at the café down the street from your office? And, Dad, I have Rome with me. He said, 'No problem.'" Then she said, "OK, we will see you in a half hour?"

Good. We met her father at the restaurant. He hugged her and kissed her on the head then he shook my hand. "So, you're the young man that got my girl's heart," he said.

"Yes, sir, and I would like your permission to have her heart forever."

He looked at me like he was going to jump. He was this big man with big feet and hands. He could have crushed me right then if he wanted to.

"Nothing is wrong, is it? You all haven't known each other that long. Is there something else I should know?"

"No, Dad. He has been the perfect gentleman. He loves me," Bianca said.

"I could believe that. Like I love your mother, even to this day."

I wanted to ask him why was he not with her but, remembering the situation that Bianca told me, I let it go and waited for his answer. "What did your mother say?" he asked.

"We haven't told her yet. Your daughter just gave me a 'yes' a couple of hours ago. Since we were in Ohio, we wanted to get your blessing."

"You seem like a nice young man and what you did for your mom was touching. It shows that you are a caring man and that is what my little girl needs since I can't be with her like I would like to. Yes, you have my blessings. Take care of my girls. Let me know what you want me to do."

"We will." I shook his hand. "I won't let you down. If you can keep it quiet, we want to tell the mothers. We will be in Ohio until Sunday. We will let them know before we leave."

"That sounds like a good idea. You know those mothers."

That I did. I also knew that we had to go ring shopping. I wanted her to pick her ring out herself since it was something I hoped she would never take off. I knew just the place. That would be on our agenda on Saturday, keeping it a secret from the moms until then. Mom did not believe in people sleeping in the same room if they were not married. She was old school like that. Ms. B slept in my sister's room. I had no clue where my sister was. I slept in my old room which was now the laundry room.

Knowing that Bianca was exhausted, she took her shower and went straight to bed. I soon followed. We had a good day and a lot to tell the moms. My head hit the pillow and I was out.

The next morning Mom was up early with breakfast all laid out and smelling so good. I went to the basement restroom to take my shower just in case Ms. B was taking her shower before breakfast.

When I came up for breakfast she was already at the table, filling her plate. This woman was so beautiful. I felt like the luckiest man in the world. Just to really see how she reacted with my mom added a special reason to marry her. It was very important to me that Mom and who ever I married have a good relationship because I planned on only doing this one time.

After breakfast, we rushed off to my favorite jewelry store in the mall. When I was younger and hanging out at the mall with the fellows, we would pass by this jewelry store, but I never thought that I would be buying something from them, especially rings. I as nervous as we walked in the door. We were greeted by a sales clerk asking how they could help us. The sales clerk was friendly and just so happened to be a man. It was good that he was pleasant because I needed help. "Let me guess," he said. "You are here to get this princess something special."

"Yes," Bianca said with much excitement. "He asked me to marry him and I said yes!"

We all had a good laugh at the way Ms. B was holding her hand out like a princess wanting to be kissed, which I did do. We picked out a nice gold engagement ring with five diamonds around the band

and a pearl in the middle. That was what she wanted. Then a plain gold wedding band for both of us.

After everything was all taken care of I could not wait to put that ring on her finger. So, right in the store, which was not very crowded, I got on my knees in front of my queen and said, "Will you marry me and live in my kingdom for the rest of your life?"

As the tears streamed down her face, I grabbed her hand and we both shook like a ninety-year-old person trying to hold a fork. I placed the engagement ring on her finger and then whispered in her ear, "Till death do us part."

The she whispered back, "Me too."

It was done. The first chapter of our lives had just begun and it felt good. I had no doubt the mothers would give us their blessings, even though we only knew each other for a short time. But this felt right. We would take our time to actually make plans for the wedding but now we had a commitment to each other.

Heading back to Mom's house, we had the giggles like little kids. She looked so good and her smile was contagious. I could tell how everywhere we went she was being admired but she was my woman, someone I was very proud of.

Heading to Mom's and talking about how we would Skype her mom and tell them at the same time, I could tell she was a little nervous. So was I but I was cool. We had her father's blessing. I didn't think we would have a problem with the moms. They knew we was crazy about each other.

When we arrived, Mom was in the kitchen. "Hey, Mom, come here for a minute. Bianca wants to call her mom so that we could all say hello."

Mom came with no trouble. Bianca kept her hand in her pocket until we got her mom on Skype. We did some small talk, asking how she was and what a good time we were having and that Mrs. Nadia was allowing us to reveal her and so on. "That's great," she said and she asked my mom how she was doing and so on. Then Bianca took her hand out of her pocket.

She put it up to the phone and said, "Rome asked me to marry him. What do you think?"

Both our moms seemed to be so happy for us and started asking questions. But, before they could ask the one of when, I said we were not rushing the wedding.

"I want to get the information out about the angel reveal and Ms. B has some things she needs to do," I said. "So, we will talk about a date and all of that at another time."

I wanted her mom to know just in case she didn't know that I loved Bianca and I would not do her wrong in any way.

My mom reassured her that I would or else I would have to deal with her. Now it was some more people we had to tell. I had not talked to Ms. Lambkin for a while. She crossed my mind from time to time but I never picked up the phone to call her, being so wrapped up in my own world. I was disappointed in myself for not staying in touch with her.

I went off to another room to give her a call while the mothers and Ms. B did their thing that women do. "Hello, Ms. Lambkin?" I said but before I could get the entire name out I realized that this was not her. She had a soft voice. This was a loud decimal tone of a voice. "No, I will get her for you."

I just assumed Ms. Lambkin would answer the phone so I just started talking. I apologized to the person before they put Ms. Lambkin on the phone. "Hey, how are you? Before you give me heck for not hearing from me, I am so sorry."

"It's OK. I know that you are a busy young man. I am not angry, just glad to hear from you right now."

I asked if she had time to talk since she had company. "No, it's OK," she said. "We can talk."

I told her about how Mrs. Nadia said yes that I could use her name to reveal the bus stop angel and that I found a young lady that I was in love with and I asked her to be my wife. "You have been busy, haven't you?" she said. "I am so happy for you and glad to hear about the reveal. When will you do the reveal, and are you going to do it in Ohio or New York?"

"It was important to Nadia's husband. Josh said that we must have the reveal in Cleveland because this is where it happened and, of course, thinking of his wife."

"You got him to loosen up? Can you believe it?"

"Well, it was my girl that loosened him up. Then I told her the situation about Mom and how everyone helped Bianca update Mom's kitchen."

"That's her name?"

"Yes, and she is so nice."

"I look forward to meeting her someday."

"I was hoping that you can be with me when I do the reveal because without you this would not have happened."

"I would love to be with you. Cinnamon High played a big role in this too, don't forget."

"There you go again, always pointing me in the right direction. I will talk with Mrs. Nadia and Josh and we will set something up for next month. I have to go back to New York for work but I do have some more time coming up. It was good talking to you. I will keep you posted."

"OK. Until then, tell your mom and Ms. Nadia and family I said hello and I look forward to seeing them."

It was time to head back to our jobs and life in the big city. Bianca called her father to tell him she would be back around the end of October to do the reveal.

We made it back safely. Ms. B's mom was so glad to see her and gave me a big hug but she had this look on her face of uncertainty. As I looked at her something hit me. For the first time, I thought about Ms. B, all that she had going, and how much she loved being with her mom. What would happen to her when we married? I took her aside and reassured her she would always be with us wherever we go until she decided to move on.

Nothing else had to be said. Her demeanor changed to relief and then I really got a hug from her. I was concerned for all my ladies that were in my life. Making it back to my apartment, I looked around at the bachelor pad. Would I miss it?

Was I really ready for marriage? All of these questions in my head but then my heart said, "Yes. I loved this lady and wanted to grow up and old with her. Our age didn't matter. If we married that same day we got engaged, I would feel the same way."

I took a shower and slept like a baby, looking forward to going to work and sharing my weekend with my boss.

I told her what happened about the lady at the bus stop being willing to be revealed but I had to do it in Ohio.

She did not have a problem with it and since I had so much vacation time, once I caught up on my work load, I had her blessing to go but to put a plug in for our little publishing company. Even though it was small, we produced good work and writers came to us.

Part 3

THE BUS STOP
ANGEL REVEAL

CHAPTER
16

BIG REVEAL

As Ms. B and I hung out we just enjoyed each other's company. She knew I had a lot on my mind so we stayed away from the wedding plans. We were sure the mommas had that covered anyway.

We talked about the best way to get Mrs. Nadia's name out there as our secret angel and make sure she was not hurt or disappointed. She came up with an idea to send a copy of the book to Mr. Billings at News Channel Seventy-Eight and explain to him that we have someone who agreed to be revealed as the Bus Stop Angel and see if he could help us set it up at the very bus stop, if it is still there.

That was a good idea. I did just what she said the next week, nervously waited and hoping he would think that this was a good story and a good idea. Ms. B did remind me that he probably was busy and had no time to read it yet. "Be patient. If it's meant to be it will be or we will try something else," she said.

She was good at that, just like Mom and Ms. Lambkin. It seemed that all the ladies in my life had my back. I realized that I didn't have too many men in my life. Me and my dad called each other from time to time but we didn't have a great relationship.

I was becoming good friends with the manager at the deli but I knew nothing about him. I had my few buddies in Ohio, which we talked from time to time about our lives. They were doing well and trying to find their way in life the only way that they knew how. My work load was heavy but I always made time for my girl and sometimes her mom would come along. Her mom was not interested in dating anyone. She still had hope that one day Bianca's father's situation would change. To get my mind off not hearing anything from Mr. Billings, it was time for a surprise for my girl. Something I started and enjoyed doing for her.

I told the manager of the Artisan Lounge, where Bianca and the Divas played, that we were engaged and asked if we could give her a surprise party just for her with her friends at the lounge. He was puzzled. "Don't other people give you both an engagement party?" he asked. He was correct but this was just for my girl to show her my appreciation for the respect and kindness she gave me.

He got that and said, "No problem. When and what do you want me to do?"

"You just open the door and we will handle everything down to the cleaning afterward."

Telling her mom and friends what I had in mind, they went to work while keeping it quiet. I called home to see if Mom wanted to come and visit. She said, "No but I'm sure your sister would love to come. She's back in town."

"Sure. I would love to see her and I am sure Ms. B would be delighted to see her again since we missed her when we were home."

Things went as planned. I got the same caterers who catered at the mansion and hired a band so that her friends could enjoy the party. Her mother told her that they were going to have a girl's night out and that she could not spend all her weekends with me. She called to say she was hanging out with her mom Friday night. "You didn't have plans, did you?" she asked.

"Oh no," I said. "Hang out with your mom. I will find something to do."

The Artisan Lounge was set up beautifully with her favorite flowers and all her friends were there. I knew that this would make her happy. She and her mom walked into the room. When the music started playing she locked her eyes on me and said, "What is this?"

"This is for you. Thank you for your support. Tonight is your night."

We had a good time and, like I said, she was glad to see my sister. We talked about that party the entire weekend. What fun we had.

My sister stayed until Sunday. We took her to the deli to hang out and she got to know the people who worked there a little better. This was my world and it was getting filled with good people who believed in me and cared for me. This was living.

My sister left for home with lots of pictures to show Mom. It had been a while now since I sent my book and question to Mr. Billings at Channel 78 but heard nothing so I was going with my back-up plan to put it out on YouTube and we would do it from the school. I ran that by all the ladies and was told to just wait a little while longer. They were sure I would hear something one way or another. Then I could go forward with the school idea.

It was mid-October and the weather was beautiful in New York. My mom said it was in Ohio too. It would be the perfect time. Something about the fall seemed to get the best out of people.

That same thought gave me hope. I had a good story and people were still buying the book. I checked in with Mom in Ohio to see if Mr. J. J. Billings had contacted her about the reveal, just in case he missed me. She informed me that he had not and that she was spreading the word that I was up to something. I didn't want to say too much until we knew all the details.

Several days after talking to Mom, I received the phone call I was waiting for; a voice I heard on the television for years: Mr. J. J. Billings from Channel 78 WGPC. He apologized for taking so long to get back with me.

He had shared my information with his boss who read the book also and thought that November, right before Thanksgiving, would be a great time, with the holidays coming and the craziness the world was in. I agreed and told him that I would talk to the other people who were involved and contact him right away.

Things were rolling. I wanted to pick a time and date that would be convenient for everyone. I spoke to everyone and they also thought that November would be a great time. This meant that Mr. Billings would interview Ms. Nadia and would talk to the city about using the same bus stop. I was not sure if the corner store was still standing or not, so I made a call to see and, behold, it was still open.

I reminded the storeowner, Mr. Knuckles, who I was and what my plans were. He was on board. I was glad that he was all for it.

With everyone on board and in their various capacities getting things set up, we knew that time would fly by so fast. We definitely wanted this to be a positive experience for everyone.

Bianca's friends at the deli were upset that I chose Ohio because they couldn't come. I did invite the manager to be with us that week. He wouldn't have to worry about a thing. I would make sure he was taken care of. He was overjoyed and said he would love to attend. He had never been to Ohio and this would be a treat for him.

Mr. Billings called me about setting up an interview at the station that Monday morning, discussing the book so that the viewers would know what the reveal was all about. This was a good idea. We set that up for November 17th, 2016 on the morning show.

This was getting to be bigger than I expected. I was kind of shy so being on the television made me a little nervous when I thought about it, but it was what I had to do. Ms. Nadia deserved it.

I arrived at the station dressed nicely but not over dressed in a suit and tie. That would be too much for me to handle. Mr. Billings brought out a copy of the book and said to the viewers how he enjoyed reading it.

He asked questions like, "what inspired you to write it?" And "how did it change your life?" And so on. I answered as clear as I could because I wanted the viewers to understand that there were many people out in the world doing good but never getting recognized. It was important to me that this lady got recognized because she changed so many people lives by her unselfishness.

The interview went well. Before I could finish the interview, people were calling in wanting to know where they could get a copy of the book. He announced all the different bookstores that carried it and, of course, online.

After the interview, Rick, Bianca's boss, and I hung out. We went to see downtown and I also introduced him to my hood. Rick was in awe with Cleveland. This was his first time visiting. He asked why I left and if I would ever consider moving back there. I told him that it had crossed my mind once to come back and open my own publishing company, but with Ms. B in my life, I would have to see what would happen.

CHAPTER
17

THE VETERAN'S LETTER

Everything turned out to be beautiful. It was around seven a.m. Everything was set at the bus stop by the Boys and Girls Club. I would never forget the experience that changed my life by that bus stop: the number fourteen going downtown Cleveland, Ohio.

People were everywhere. We got a really good turnout. As Mr. Billings did the broadcast he said, "This is what we have all been waiting for. Here she is!" At that time, Nadia came out of the corner store to the bus stop.

There were cheers and people saying, "Yes, that's the lady!" It seemed that some of the people who wrote the letters were present to witness this. She was a little nervous but, like her, she was very humble.

She told Mr. Billings how she wanted to make a difference in as many lives as she could but did not want any praise for it. This was her life calling. After a few more questions, which she answered beautifully, the interview ended with Mr. Billings saying, "Be careful how you treat strangers. They just might turn out to be an angel in disguise."

People came up to get her autograph and some asked her if she remembered them., One lady said that she was the lady at the dollar store and she never forgot Ms. Nadia and what she did for her that day. Another person came up saying that she was nice to her brother on the bus. He had kidney failure and knew he was dying but she gave him a smile and offered him candy. He died but he never forgot.

People were coming up one after another. Her husband stood by her side and told the people that they thanked them for coming out and their kindness. It was time for Mrs. Nadia to get some rest, which was true. She had a good and stressful morning.

As we got in our cars, I rode with Josh and Ms. Nadia, asking if could I take them to breakfast. I wasn't sure if they had time to eat because it was early. Bianca and Mom was following us. Nadia's mom had someone take her home right before it was over. She was probably tired. He said, "No, I think we better go home. She needs some rest."

He knew her mom probably had breakfast ready for her. Which was so true. We pulled up to their house and some of the neighbors were coming out the front door. Yes, they had brought anything that you could have wanted for breakfast. The house was loaded.

Josh suggested that I call my mom and the others to come over and eat with them. "With all of this food, we could never eat it all," he said. I did as he said they all came. We feasted and afterward Mrs. Dixon told us to feel free to find a spot to rest. She knew we were exhausted and full.

She brought out blankets, pillows, and sleeping bags. We took her up on it. Ms. B and I found a cozy spot in the dining room. It was good to see her and hold her in my arms again, and I could tell that she felt the same. It was around ten a.m. and the house was quiet except the few sounds of our bodies letting out relief.

My cell phone buzzed. I had cut it off because I didn't want to wake anyone. I whispered to the person on the other end. "Hello?" I said. It was Mr. Billings who said that he had just received a letter by e-mail from a veteran at the Veterans Administration Hospital. He said what Ms. Nadia did for him and wanted me to give her the letter. I couldn't wait until everyone was awake. The aroma of coffee woke them up. Ready or not. You couldn't sleep through that. My mom and Ms. Nadia's mom had coffee and finger sandwiches ready in case we were hungry, like we had not eaten enough for breakfast. As we all wiped away sleep and saliva to get some of that good coffee,

I told them about my phone call and how I had Mr. Billings e-mail the letter to me. I read it to the crowd:

The Stranded Veteran

Here I am again at the Veterans Hospital in Cleveland, Ohio, which I have spent many days of my life since I came from Iraq. Now I live in one of the apartments that was built for us veterans who were homeless and I was one of those. I wasn't sure if I had family or not. After I came home I couldn't find anyone I knew. I had no parents because they passed away while I was in the army. All I knew was that I had a brother. I don't know what happened to him but he wasn't in Ohio.

I often thought of a situation I was in some years back. At that time, I was living on the west side of Cleveland and I had to get the shuttle bus to get to the east side VA for the treatment that I needed. The bus came at a certain time of morning and you had to be ready or they would leave you. It only came on Mondays, Wednesdays, and Fridays, so I had to get it. I was in pain. I had shrapnel in my right arm. The VA on the east side had this special treatment that eased my pain for a while.

I remember I rushed out to get the bus that Wednesday morning. I made it to the VA and was told to be out front by four o'clock or I would miss the bus and it would not be back until Friday

Morning. I had a few dollars to eat while I was at my appointment, so I knew I could not miss the bus. I knew no one in Cleveland and had no money.

Well, I missed the bus. I don't know what happened. I was at the stop at 3:45 p.m. I specifically looked at the old watch my daddy gave me when I was a boy. Worried about what to do, I went back inside to ask if the bus came early and was told that it was now 4:15 p.m. That old watch decided to stop on me at the wrong time.

I was stuck and, back then, the VA could not do anything to help me. I was so upset that I could not get back home; I looked around the area to see where I might have a chance to sleep for the night without someone bothering me. I had heard about the gang problem in Cleveland and I was hoping not to be one of their victims. I sat at the bus stop with my bag. It was a little cold out but I had enough sense to bring my coat.

The city bus came by, dropping people off and picking people up, but no one asked me where I was going or if I needed help. I'm sure when they looked at me they thought I was out for trouble but I was just a bit confused. I'm sure the war played with my head a bit. I was on medication. It had to be about five o'clock because workers from inside the VA were coming out, getting in cars and a few catching the bus.

They had to see that something was wrong but no one bothered to say anything to me and, with my fuzzy mind and probably pride, I said nothing to them. Then I was all alone. The bus had left. The cars were gone and I sat there with my last cigarette. Then there she came, walking up the street, smiling, and asking how I was doing. I was so glad to talk to someone. I found myself telling her what happened to me.

She looked a bit young, so I didn't think she could do anything, but if she could give me a few dollars I could walk a couple of blocks and at least get something to eat and find me a spot to sleep.

She said, "I'm sorry. I don't know anyone that can take you home but, here, get yourself something to eat." She gave me enough money to get me something to eat and I was able to find a cheap hotel room for the night. Remembering that day so well in my mind, this woman rescued me and seeing her on television was a great joy to me. I thought I would never see her again to say thank you and to let her know that I am hanging in there. So, yes, she is an Angel. She was mine that day.

What a letter and what an adventure this was for all the parties involved, especially Mrs. Nadia. I'm sure many people are all over the world doing random acts of kindness but this one touched and changed my life in a way that I could never imagine.

I would probably get more letters about this lady. Better yet, they could give them directly to the source. This is my story and I found my angel.

Part 4

THE LETTERS

SATURDAY MORNING SMILE

It was early on a Saturday as I looked down the street at the bus stop. I saw one person standing there. As I got closer I was met with the biggest smile. I could have come to kidnap her or hurt her. A young lady out by herself at five a.m. could have been in big trouble and she smiles as though she was so glad to see me. She was in luck because I wasn't out to hurt anyone.

She said, "good morning" and told me how glad she was to see me and how she had to be at work so early on a Saturday. She was so understanding and I talked about my job and having to look for another one because my job was moving out of the city.

You can tell she felt so bad for my situation. After a few minutes the bus came and she said, "I hope I see you tomorrow. I have to work Sunday too." As we got on the bus I watched her as she sat still smiling at anyone who would look her way.

I had never met anyone like her before, so I kind of looked forward to seeing her on Sunday.

This time I came a little earlier hoping we would have more time to talk because I liked talking to her. It was not about a relationship because I knew this lady had to have somebody.

When I arrived at the bus shelter, there she stood smiling, and greeted me with her usual "good morning." She explained how the job went on Saturday and how late she got home. As we were talking, she put something in my hand and said, "Pay it forward when you get a chance." It was like she knew what was going on in my mind. I wanted a pack of cigarettes so bad, but

I only had bus fare for the rest of the week. Asking my old lady for money was not the best for me. I thanked her and told her I would see her again but that was the last I saw of her and no one has ever given me anything since. And I do need to pay it forward because I have a new job.

DOLLAR STORE CHRISTMAS GIFTS

I was running in the dollar store a week before Christmas with the last few dollars I had. I still needed to get something for my mother. I had taken care of the kids. They didn't get much because this was one of the worst Christmases that I had since I had been in Cleveland.

I came here from Boston. I thought the people was stingy there but I was wrong. The people in Cleveland would not give you "eye water to cry with" I heard my grandmother say one day. I was trying not to get anything from the state. I had a little job and was trying to go to school to be a STNA.

When I came into the store, looking to see what I could get, the cell phone rings. It was my mother saying she needed something. I must have got loud because everybody looked my way. "I ain't got no money," I said. I didn't mean to come at Mom like that but she was stressed to the limit.

I knew I hurt her feelings. Before she hung up she said she was sorry but didn't know how sorry I was to come at her like that.

After I hung up with Mom someone tapped me on the shoulder. "I heard your conversation," she said. Before I could get mad about her coming at me, she put something in my hand and said, "Pay it forward when you get a chance." I thanked her and got what my mother wanted and something for myself. I told my mom and friends about this experience. It only happened once but I can stop saying that the people in Cleveland want to give you eye water to cry with. She gave me a smile.

STNA Worker

I'm already an old lady and I should have taken care of my finances in my younger years. I didn't so now I am working with these clients at my age and they are not very nice. I walked slowly to the bus stop. That was all I could do. Even though one bus stop was closer to my client's home I had to go where I could sit. I sat there wondering what I was going to do because that lady was so mean to me.

I was tired, hungry, and just beat down. I was also disappointed in myself for not looking out when I was younger. I now lived with my sister and was trying to help out, so I had to work.

I knew the bus would be there soon so I tried to dry the tears. When I looked up I saw this smiling face. "Good morning," she said. She didn't know how much I needed to see a smiling face at that time.

It made the entire world of difference. We began to talk until her bus arrived. She had to run but, before she ran off, she handed me a plastic bag. When I opened it, it had candy wrappers of different colors. As I opened a beautiful red wrapper, the taste of cherry pleased my palate. Then I saw a white strip of paper in the bag. I was curious to see what was on it. It was a nice note that said, "You can make it." How did she know? I had some things troubling me; those words were right on time.

Now I understand something. When I looked up and saw her face, I could see a light shining so bright and if I had the chance to thank her again I would. I have taken some steps to make my life better and I want my light to shine like hers.

GETTING PIZZA

Getting pizza was not one of my things. My kids was grown and out on their own. My wife had passed away recently and I had no one to cook for me or to cook for. So, I called in a pizza and, as I went to pick it up, I thought about how much I missed my Mary. She was the love of my life. There was nothing about her that didn't make me happy. I knew I would never find another woman like her.

She gave me forty-two beautiful years. All of our kids was successful and respectful. Nothing like you see today. These young folks, and some old folks, have no respect for themselves or their elders.

As I walked into the Pizza Parlor to pick up the pizza that I called in earlier, I saw that it had a nice crowd waiting. So, I figured that, even though I called it in, it might be a wait. Several of the patrons were complaining about how slow things were and asking how long before their order would be up. It did not matter to me. I had nothing but time. I was glad to get out of the housed and get some fresh air.

I noticed a young lady sitting and smiling my way. I didn't know her and, with the mental state I was in, I didn't want to get to know her. If she was looking for a sugar daddy it would not be me. I smiled back and then she started a conversation. Not wanting to be rude, I joined in the conversation. By that time everyone had their orders and left.

We began to talk more now about so many things and I ended up telling her about how I had lost my wife and how it was so hard and everything about my life and my kids. After she listened she began to tell me how I would meet someone and how my wife would want me to and that I would be happy again.

This lady talked some stuff that me and my wife had talked about. I could not take it. I cried at that point. I was glad no one else was in there. I was a grown man and I did not know this lady, but she touched me deeply. By then her pizza was up. As she went to get it I saw her beauty better. Her heart was so beautiful. I wanted to ask her for a hug but I didn't have the nerves. Then she said, "Give me a hug."

I hugged her and cried. She wanted to tell me her name but I said "no." I knew she belonged to someone. She reminded me so much of my wife. I said, "I'll see you again" hoping I would but I did not. I am now sorry I did not get her name.

UMBRELLA

On a sunny day, I decided to go to the museum to see the beautiful old stones from back in time. When I came out it looked a little cloudy but the sun was shining so bright. I thought I would take a chance and not take an umbrella. I wouldn't stay that long, just in case. I got lost in the beauty and stayed later than expected. When I looked out to go home it was raining. I had enough sense to bring a raincoat at least.

As I walked outside rain was sprinkling, so I began to walk a little faster. A car pulled up beside me and someone stuck an umbrella out of the window and said, "I don't need it. You do." They drove away before I could say thank you. I was not able to look up if I wanted to see who it was. Due to my arthritis, I could not straighten up my back. I could lift my head and smile.

I don't know. Maybe she rides the bus regularly and just happened to have gotten a ride to the museum. I, too, have never been given anything in seventy years of life and I, too, say thank you. I will pass that umbrella on to someone else who needs it. I have plenty but am glad I had an encounter with the angel too.

Saved My Life

I was rushing, like always, trying to get to my doctor's appointment. Seemed as though the bus driver decided to slow poke around on one of the worst days for me. The weather was not that bad. At the VA hospital it was not easy to get an appointment and I could not miss this one.

As the bus stopped I rushed off and headed to the crosswalk. The light was yellow, not that this was a major street during rush hour. I looked at the light and when a voice said, "Be careful." Just as I looked back, while stepping off the curve, a car swooshed by. She pulled me back right on time.

"Thank you," I said while looking at the light and hoping that it would change soon. The only thing on my mind was getting to my appointment on time.

When it did, I dashed off and made my appointment right on time. I thought about what this lady had done. She saved my life. I would not need a doctor's appointment or any other kind of appointment. Grateful to be alive, I had another appointment coming up and I was going to take the earlier bus this time. I'd rather be early than late.

As I got on the bus, I thought about the lady who saved my life but I would not remember her. There were so many ladies on the bus when a voice said, "Remember me?"

"Oh yeah, you are that lady from the other day."

I told her how I was taking the earlier bus this time so that I would not be late. I smiled because I felt so comfortable talking to this person.

We got off at the same stop again. This time she said, "Listen to this," and she gave me a CD player with earphones.

"OK," I said. I had little time. As I listened it was gospel music. She ran on and I said, "Wait, you left your CD player."

She said, "That's yours."

Here she goes again saving my life. As I got to my appointment, I was early enough to sit down and listen to the CD. It was some good down-home singing. It made my day and changed my life. I slow down more and listen to the music. I've since bought more gospel CDs. My health is better and I am enjoying life a little more.

High School Girl

The bus was crowded and we girls were loud like girls are. School started at eight so that didn't give me enough time to eat breakfast that day. I rushed out of the house to get the bus and meet my girls. "I am so hungry. I didn't get a chance to get breakfast. Anybody got something to eat?" I asked.

"I got a candy bar," one of my girls said.

"OK."

I was glad my girl had something that I could put in my stomach. One time, in science class, the boy sitting next to me had his stomach growling so loud that everybody laughed at him. He was so embarrassed and I did not want that to happen to me.

We laughed and were loud the whole time on the bus. Everybody kept looking back at us with mean looks. I knew we were getting a little too loud for that time of the morning, but, being in our own little world, I know that the other girls thought nothing of it. We were not disrespectful but I am sure we were annoying.

We didn't curse or anything. We was just being girls. This one lady on the bus looked back at us and smiled. I said to myself, "At least that lady understands."

The bus driver had reached my destination and I noticed that it was where the woman was getting off also. She came up right behind me and, as we reached the bus shelter, she said, "Here. Take this and get yourself some lunch." I took the money that she gave me and thanked her. I caught up with the other girls and told them what just happened. Of course, no one does that kind of stuff and no one had ever done that for me.

I knew she was cool. I was able to buy me a snack before class. I looked for her the next day, not for money, but to make sure I said, "thank you" but I never saw her again.

SO EMBARRASSED

I was in the grocery store on a Saturday afternoon picking up some things that was needed and wanted at home. My husband was in the car. I was the only one in the line at the time. As the cashier was ringing up my groceries, it looked like things were more than I had added up as I went.

By the time the cashier finished ringing up all my groceries, I was a bit short. By this time, the line behind me was long and I was so embarrassed. I didn't want to put anything back because of my embarrassment. "This never happens to me," I said. I called my husband in the car to see what he had. He didn't have much money on him. It was not enough. What was I going to do? I had no choice but to put somethings back. I was afraid to look back at the people behind me. I knew they were agitated because I used to get that way myself.

"OK," I said to the clerk. "I will run out to the car."

She looked at me like I was crazy. "Are you kidding me? Look at this line."

Just then, a voice said, "How much does she need?" She looked at the amount and said, "I got it."

"Are you sure?" I asked, being polite, but I was glad someone rescued me. "This never happens. Can I give you a hug?"

I hurried out of that store to tell my husband what happened and, because of that experience, I will be more understanding in any aisle from now on. I don't know if this is the same person but this was an experience I will never forget. And, yes, she did have a big smile on her face.

TWO DOLLAR FIX

I was strung out from the night before, getting my hands on whatever I could to just feel like I was alive. My day-to-day quest was to score from anybody, anyhow I could, even if that meant knocking them in the head for a few dollars. My dad was a cop and my mom a council woman to keep their good name and status. I figured I could get away with it as long as I didn't kill anyone.

I don't know how I got in that predicament. My parents gave me and my siblings anything that they could to make our lives better. I was such a disappointment to them but I thought I could handle it. Boy, was I wrong.

This thing had me. My parents tried to get me help several times but I would walk out of every place they put me in. They didn't understand. I was just as tired of myself as they were tired of me. I wanted to shake it but I couldn't.

Everyone on the street knew me and knew that I would steal at the wink of an eye. So, of course, no one trusted me to be around unless I had money or some stuff. Anything. It didn't matter. This one morning, I saw someone I had never seen before in this big, red, floppy hat, sitting at the bus stop early in the morning. Was this person crazy or bold? She was taking a big chance being dressed in a way that stood out. At that particular area where the bus stop was located was not the safest bus shelter for her to be in. People had been robbed there in the past. You could tell that she had not a care in the world. She was just going her merry way.

I made my way over, ready to shoot my usual. Feel the person out and see what I could take while getting away. I lifted up that big, red, floppy hat and saw the biggest smile coming back at me. I took a different approach. Why? I cannot tell you. That move I made to push her hat away could have gotten me killed from many others on the street.

"You got a dollar?" I asked. As she reached in her coat pocket to give me a dollar she smiled and, without a word, gave it to me. So, I pushed my luck and said, "You got two dollars?"

No questions asked she reached in her pocket and gave me another one. This was too easy. As I asked for another she said, "OK. Now, you asked for a dollar and I gave you two. That's all I have."

I knew she had more but I didn't want to hurt her. "OK," I said as I walked away, seeing one of my homies across the street.

I should have asked for ten dollars the first time. I think she would have given it to me. "You look cute any-way," I said as I hurried across the street.

My life didn't change but I didn't forget that day. I do ask for a couple of dollars from people now but no one pays me any attention.

THE LONELY YOUNG MAN

I know I looked a mess as I got on the bus and looked around. I could tell no one wanted me to sit next to them. To stay out of trouble, I looked for a seat where I could be by myself. Scared, lonely, and hungry, I had chosen this lifestyle that my family did not understand.

They gave me a choice: to change my ways or I would have to move out. I had nowhere to go so I tried my best to act like what they wanted me to be: a teenage boy. But it just didn't work for me. Pretty soon they heard about my life and the things I was doing. My family put me out with just the clothes on my back.

"How could they do this to me?" I thought, "Don't they love me?"

I found myself lying under bridges, like so many other people, but my father was a pastor. This one morning, I was walking along just trying to figure out what to do next. I saw one of the guys who slept under the bridge with me. He had a bus pass he got from somewhere. Back then they were bus transfers and you could only use it one time.

I could ride the bus downtown and back for a while. I looked up and this lady got on the bus. She looked my way and smiled. I smiled back, anxious to have some human contact in any way I could. She sat next to me and started a conversation about the weather and so on. People were staring. We were laughing and just having the best conversation that I had in a long time with someone looking me in the eye.

Well, I got up at the next stop. "It was good talking to you," she said. I wanted so much to ask her for some

change but I was too embarrassed with everyone looking at us. Instead she reached into her bosom and took
out some money and gave it to me, then smiled and got
off of the bus.

HAND WARMERS

My mommy told me about the letter in the newspaper. I wanted to let you know that a lady at the bus stop helped me and my mommy. My hands was so cold waiting for the bus. This lady came up and gave me and my mommy some hand warmers. I was so glad because I was so cold.

THE BEGGAR

"Hey, lady, do you have a food stamp card? I need something to eat. I ain't got no money."

I knew when I went into the grocery store that I had no money but my stomach needed something in it. I had spent the little money I had on what I always do and, each month, I suffered for it.

I went to the food bank several times already. They got hip to my game. This time I really needed some food. I looked around the grocery store with intent to take something while my partner was on the other side of the store trying to see what he could get. This time I took a chance and asked. I did not want to go back to jail. It was a Sunday, so I figured the church folks were in a giving mood.

This was the only lady that had a smile on her face as I approached her. "No," she said, "I don't have a food stamp card but, here, get yourself something to eat."

I thanked her and told her about me and my partner when he showed up. "Come on, man," I said. "This nice lady hooked us up."

He, too, thanked her. As we walked away she said, "Pass it on when you get yourself together."

I told her I would. I don't know if she was driving or on the bus but no one has ever since given me a thing. I tried that same thing over and over but they just looked at me like I was crazy.

I either had to get myself together and hold on to some of my disability check or steal. I have not changed my behavior but I will never forget that lady.

LADY BUS DRIVER

It was one of those days. I did not want to come to work. My bus route was changed on one of the craziest days. The bus seemed to be extra crowded this day and the rudest people seemed to be riding all morning.

One of my stops was right in front of a grocery store. I didn't have time to take a break and it was time for the five o'clock crowd. I had a little breakfast to hold me over until I took my break. My relief called in to the company saying that he would be a couple of hours late.

That meant that, at the end of this five o'clock run, I could get a quick break. One problem: the restaurants and stores were a little distance away. I couldn't leave the bus and go over and get anything to eat. "Oh well," I thought. I could hold out another couple of hours. I could lose a few pounds anyway.

Stopping by the grocery store, nodding as people got on, it was already crowded so people had to squeeze in and stand because all the seats were taken. This one lady got on and said, "hello" with a big smile. This was unusual for me, so I gladly smiled back and said, "hello."

I was sorry she had to stand but she didn't seem to mind. I looked in the mirror and she had that same smile on her face as if it was painted on. Soon it was time for her to get off the bus. She stopped and handed me a bag and said, "I know you get hungry. Here, I bought you something."

I thanked her and said I was going to my break and I would enjoy it. I had no idea what it was but I was so grateful and I wondered how she knew.

THE WIDOWER

I, like so many senior citizens, was having a rough time making ends meet. It was almost time to replenish my almost empty refrigerator. I was trying to get the things I needed, like eggs, bread, and some meat (which I didn't eat much). It was a week before I would receive my pension check, so the few dollars I had in my pocket had to keep me together for a while.

My wife passed away five years ago and the only son we had also passed two years ago. I had outlived everybody. That doesn't mean that this was a good thing for me.

I had my church family but, in this church, most of the members were elderly like me. It was an old school church. The young people were not coming except occasionally with their grandparents.

As I was picking up things and looking at the prices I had to put them right down. The store wasn't that crowded so I did not have to rush for being in any one's way. While looking in the frozen food aisle, I thought maybe I would get one of those key-lime pies but I had to get other things first. Then I would see.

I glanced up to see this young lady smiling at me. I smiled back but with concern. What did she want? I was old and you could look at me and see that I didn't have much to offer.

I walked on to another aisle. It seemed like she was following me or just happened to be shopping in the same aisles I was in. Then it happened. She came closer to where I was. My heart was pounding. Was she going to ask me for money?

She said, "Here, I want to give you something." I opened my hand and accepted what was in her hand. It was a nice, crisp twenty-dollar bill. Before I could say, "thank you" she was gone. I looked for her but did not see her anywhere. I purchased my food and pie, went home, and thanked God for my angel.

Girl on the Way to a Job Interview

As I hurried across the street to wait for the bus, my mind was in a fog. This was my tenth interview in a year and no one called me back. I wanted to give up but I couldn't. I wasn't completely broke. I kept my father-in-law who was a stroke survivor. He paid me to do cleaning and things to help him on a daily basis.

I needed my own money. I approached the bus stop and a young lady was sitting in the bus shelter. We both said our good mornings, which felt good to me because my father-in-law was the only person I had talked to for a while.

She started a conversation asking if I was going to work. "No, a job interview," I said. Then I found myself telling her the whole story and that is not like me. You could tell she felt sympathy for me and encouraged me to not to give up. She had an experience something like mine and she found a good job.

The bus came. She got on first and I followed her and sat next to her. Now I felt safe, a little relieved, and less nervous about this interview. As we sat, nothing else was said for a while. As we rode along she turned to me and gave me a pack of gum.

She said, "I hope you will not get offended. Your breath is a little taut this morning just like mine. Here is a pack of gum."

As I reached for the gum it dawned on me, "How dare she tell me my breath stinks," then I cooled down because she did say that hers was too, which she was correct.

I thanked her and, as she came to her stop, she gave me bus fare to use for another day. Now how can you get offended when the person helps you with the problem. Who does that?

THE COOK

I was into my second month of freedom from doing a five-year sentence for petty theft in the Mansfield Ohio Penitentiary. I knew better, my parents made sure that me and my brother had our needs met.

They provided a stable home for us and things were going well, until I chose to hang out with the wrong people. I am not saying it was their fault. I made the stupid decision to hold up a store with my so-called friends and, of course, I was the one who did the hard time because I had a gun.

When I arrived at the prison, I was so scared but I had to pretend as if I was tough so that the things that I heard about in prison would not happen to me. I got lucky or something because my roommate was from my hometown of Cleveland, Ohio. We got along well enough to make my time tolerable.

When it was time for work detail, I had been a part-time cook at a restaurant. I had learned some mad skills from my mom who could cook almost anything she put her mind to. That worked out well for me. Adding what I already knew about cooking and the teaching that Big Mo, the head cook, gave me made my time go fast.

After my time, I knew the drill. In order to keep out of trouble while on parole, I had to get a job. My mother passed away while I was doing time. However, my pops was keeping it together, so I was able to move back home with him.

Not having any driver's license, I had to catch the bus for a while, which I did not care too much for but I had to do what I had to do.

This one day on the bus, I sat next to this female who seemed to be friendly. We struck up a conversation. She asked if I was going to work and what type of work that I did. Not wanting to reveal where I had just come from, I told her that I was a cook and that I was looking for employment.

Oh, that really got the conversation going since it was close to the Thanksgiving holiday. She asked, "How do you cook your dressing?"

I shared my technique with her, which she wrote down and gladly thanked me. She had reached her destination and, as she got off the bus, I hated to see her go.

We said our good byes and that was the beginning of a new mindset for me. This female was refreshing to talk to and this was the first real conversation that I had with anyone since I was out.

Figuring that I would never see her again, I focused my attention on what I had to do and that was finding a job. Several weeks had passed and I finally landed a part-time position at a sports bar with full-time potential, if things worked out.

I was feeling good about myself now. I could help dad out with the bills. It was getting close to the Christmas holiday and I was on my way to work when my angel got on the bus.

She found a seat behind me, so I had to turn around to tell her hi and that I was glad to see her.

I asked how her Thanksgiving was and she said how the recipe that I gave her was the bomb and how everyone enjoyed it. I said that I was glad to hear that, and then she gave me an envelope and said, "Happy Holidays."

I turned around and opened the envelope. She had put some money in it and a nice card. She could not see the tears in my eyes but the person next to me did. I wiped them away before I turned to her to say, "Thank you very much."

Again, we said our goodbyes.

THE GLOVES

Having my baby daddy push me away from his front door was devastating to me. I had called him several times because the baby needed some pampers and he didn't answer. I took it on myself to go over. My foster mother warned me about boys like him.

I didn't listen and it happened. I dropped out of school to raise this child. I knew better. That's why I was in foster care, because of an unfit father. I knocked on the door and some girl about my age opened the door.

I asked if he was home and, before she could say anything, I pushed my way in. He ran from the bedroom telling me to get the blank out of his house. I couldn't believe that he would do this to me. I had his child. Not wanting him to hit me like he had done before, I walked away so ashamed.

I had enough bus fare to get back home, but no gloves or scarf. Just a coat because I thought I was going to hang out with him and he would take me home. I was so wrong.

When I got to the bus stop a lady was there. She smiled and said, "hi" but I did not have a smile in me. She might have sensed it so she turned away and said nothing else. I was hoping that bus would hurry up. I was so cold.

This time she turned and faced me and then handed me some gloves, some nice gloves, and said, "Here, take these. I know your hands are cold. I wish I had a hat too. The bus should be coming soon."

All I heard was "the bus should be coming soon." I don't know if I thanked her but that day I needed someone who cared.

THE BOOK

I looked down the aisle for a seat when this voice said, "You can sit here."

Rushing to get to that seat, I looked toward the young lady who had the biggest smile at that time of morning.

We exchanged "good mornings" as I sat with a relief that I was next to someone nice for a change. She was reading a book so I did not want to disturb. Every now and then she would glance up to see if she was getting closer to her stop.

I wanted to ask her what she was reading, but I didn't want her to think that I was trying to make a pass at her. I believe I was old enough to be her father. Soon it was time for her to get off the bus. She said, "Excuse me," and handed me the book that she was reading. "I read this already. I think you will like it. Pass it on if you like when you finish."

I thanked her and really did not want her to get off the bus yet. I looked at the title of the book. It was an inspirational book by a Pastor Huckaback. "What a funny name," I thought. But the title was Be at Peace With Yourself, Then You Can Be at Peace With Others.

"Wow," I thought as I watched her walk away. I did feel a peaceful presence while sitting next to her. I read the book several times and it did change my life.

WOULD-BE CHURCH HOLD UP

I have no idea if this has anything to do with a bus angel or the same young lady. But what happened to me and my buddy one Sunday has never happened again. We were doing our usual getting high and talking smack.

Then this cat said the most bizarre thing that he had said in years, "Let's go to church."

"OK," I thought. "This cat is not going to rob a church."

I had done my share of robberies and hadn't got caught yet, but this I wasn't sure I would do.

Yeah, we were broke and spent our last twenty on some weed, even knowing that my girl was pregnant and needed something. But that twenty wasn't enough. "OK, man, I'm game. We both could use different scenery, plus I love that good singing and looking at the honeys."

We got to the little store front church. The singing was awesome and lot a big, leg honeys in the place. We sat in the back just watching and when you high it don't matter. Not long after getting there it was offering time. As the pastor prayed, the ushers got ready to come around. The cat was acting so nervous that he could not sit still. The next thing I knew he was headed to the front of the church. He stopped one of the ladies carrying the offering tray. Oh no, I said to myself, I hope he is not going to do anything stupid without letting me in on it. He must have asked where the restroom was because she pointed at the rear of the church.

Whatever it was, he didn't tell me. He went in the back and the usher came around. I waved at the tray and they moved on. This sister in front of me looked back and smiled then reached her hand toward me and gave me what looked like a five-dollar bill but, when I looked, it was a nice piece of change. Then she said, "Jesus loves you."

I thanked her. Now I knew my buddy better not try to rob this place. Sitting there nervous, I waited for him to come back. I reached over and whispered, "Man, we got a blessing. Let's rise up out of here."

I opened my hand so that I could see what was in it without disturbing the service. He said softly, "Who gave you that?"

He knew I was broke when I came in the door. I told him what the sister in front of me had done, and he laughed. "Man, I was in the back trying to figure out how to get the offerings and tithes."

I told him to chill and turned to enjoy some more of the service before we left. We laughed, but it was no laughing matter. I believe she was our angel that Sunday.

ABOUT THE AUTHOR

Brenda Pickett Watson was born in Selma, Alabama to Annie Mae Pickett and L. C. Butler on October 26, 1958. She is the tenth of twelve siblings. At the age of thirteen she was sent to live with her brother in Cleveland, Ohio, where she finished school and graduated in 1977. While working her first job at a movie  theatre, her mentor from her church, Mrs. Juanita Smith, informed her of a position at the Cleveland Institute of Music, and she took advantage of their services. She took vocal, conducting, and piano lessons at the preparatory school. She left after thirty-one years to help her husband, Charles Watson, of twenty-six years recover from a stroke. Brenda has sung with the Martin Luther King Community Choir at Severance Hall and orchestrated a concert at the Church of the Covenant to donate the proceeds to the Cancer program at the University Hospital Cancer Unit. Brenda has a love for children, though she has none of her own. She reaches out as often as possible to help others with their children. Brenda's motto is to "live and let live while making a difference."